An Unlikely Catechism

William Reiser, S.J.

An Unlikely Catechism

Some Challenges for the Creedless Catholic

Paulist Press *New York/Mahwah*

Acknowledgments
The lines from David Ignatow's poem "Between the Living and the Dead" from his book *Whisper to the Earth* (copyright © 1981 by David Ignatow) are quoted with the kind permission of the publisher (Little, Brown & Co., Inc., in association with The Atlantic Monthly Press). The lines of Stanza VIII from Robert Penn Warren's "American Portrait: Old Style," which appears in his book *Now and Then: Poems 1976–1978* (copyright © 1978 by Robert Penn Warren), are quoted with the kind permission of Random House, Inc.

Imprimi Potest
Very Rev. Edward M. O'Flaherty, S.J.
Provincial, Society of Jesus of New England

Library of Congress
Catalog Card Number: 85-60293

ISBN: 0-8091-2706-7

Published by Paulist Press
997 Macarthur Boulevard
Mahwah, New Jersey 07430

Printed and bound in the
United States of America

Contents

An Instruction

What makes people holy?
>Contact with the living God.

How do we touch the living God?
>By desire.

How do we learn where our desires are leading us?
>God will teach us.

How does God teach us?
>By giving us the word of life.

How do we hear the word of life?
>By faith.

How are we brought to faith?
>Through genuine communion with others.

And how is genuine communion created?
>By the Spirit of Jesus.

Introduction

Jesus, the soul, resurrection. I am not altogether sure why I keep thinking about these three realities. Perhaps the thread drawing them together is my knowledge that Jesus is the one who saves, my puzzling over exactly what about us is so valuable to God that it is worth saving, and my hope that the years spent trying to be faithful to Jesus will one day bear lasting fruit.

There are other doctrines, of course. We study the sacraments, the Trinity, the inspiration of the Bible, and so on. Reflecting on doctrines like these is what keeps theologians occupied and provides the materials for religion classes. I teach such courses. But these are not the issues which are immediately relevant to my experience as a believer. The three questions posed by Immanuel Kant, an eighteenth century German philosopher, toward the end of his book *The Critique of Pure Reason* are more to the point because they crystallize the type of questions many believers do think about. "What can I know?" "What should I do?" "What may I hope?" Kant was unable to answer the first question to his satisfaction because he had demonstrated that reality was not fully knowable by the human mind, which is all we have to work with. But he was more confident about answering the second and third questions. Kant realized that human beings were so made that they had to act uprightly if they were to be fully human, and it made little sense to live a morally good life unless there were a divine being which conferred meaningfulness upon human existence. He wrote: "Thus without a God and without a world, not visible to us now, but hoped for, the glorious ideas of morality are indeed objects of applause and admiration, but not springs of purpose and action, because they fail to fulfill all the aims which are natural to every rational being."[1]

Each of us carries around a number of unanswered religious questions. Since these questions are generally not easy to figure out, we may just tuck them away in our heads, counting on the fact that minds greater than ours have pondered them. Or else we may actually devote some time to considering them, but the answers we seek may be slow in coming, or unconvincing when they do come. In this case we might reassure ourselves that intelligent believers have been able to live their faith without discovering the answers to a number of profound, challenging questions. And if that is so, we tell ourselves, should not those of us with lesser theological skills simply believe what the Church teaches? Will our relationship to God be damaged if we leave our questions—and maybe also our doubts—in a continual state of intellectual suspension? If an Immanuel Kant, or a Karl Rahner, for that matter, finally has to admit that the mystery of God is incomprehensible, then the rest of us can at least be encouraged by the fact that such thinkers have not drawn the conclusion that God is foreign to human experience.

A few questions are so complicated, in fact, that only God could have a handle on them. For instance, how do we harmonize our belief that the fulfillment of human life lies beyond this world with our obligation to work at improving the conditions of this one? It is like asking why we bother about building, inventing, imagining, or creating anything new here in view of the fact that someday life on our planet will end, since the earth, like every planet, must perish. If the final reality is heaven, then the value of the present reality is undercut. But if the present becomes absolutely decisive, is there any proportion between here and the hereafter? Furthermore, what counts as valuable human activity? Is it work on behalf of justice and peace, feeding the hungry, loving the enemy and befriending the stranger or refugee? Then what about those whose lives have to be spent laboring in factories or at home with children—are these also activities which build the kingdom of God? Or are such people excused from devoting most of their time and energy to serving the cause of peace and justice?

Moreover, what of those in prison, or in hospitals, or in refugee camps? Are they likewise excused from the human obligation to make the world more humane, more livable, or are they bound to do what they can within the limited circumstances of a prison, a hospital, a wheelchair, an empty stomach? And how do we determine how much activity for the kingdom is necessary to win our salvation? How much does God expect of us? Is it necessary to devote one's whole life to serving Jesus and his sisters and brothers when there are many who make it into heaven by the skin of their teeth? It is spiritually taxing to work with all one's strength for a more human world while remembering at the same time that this world will not last. For, on the one hand, we have to labor as if this is the only world, the only existence we shall ever have. And yet, on the other hand, what makes the world so important in the first place? What is so valuable about human beings that we should be concerned about hunger, injustice, loneliness, or the godlessness of society, in the first place? As I mentioned, some concerns are probably best consigned to the hands of God.

"What can I know?" I can know Jesus. I can experience Jesus as the one who shows me what genuine humanness looks like. I can meet Jesus, and in this meeting I can encounter the mystery of God—a mystery which I know but remain incapable of comprehending. "What must I do?" I must become, to the degree that I can, a man or a woman who loves. But I become a person who loves only by the effort of looking for goodness in others. I must learn to see men and women as my sisters and brothers, and if they are brother and sister to me, then I must want them to live with the same freedom, dignity, and peace which I desire for my own family. The effort of loving is realized through service, through caring, and through laboring against all forms of poverty and oppression. This is how the Christian soul is formed.

"What may I hope for?" I may hope that, if I lead a decent life, my passing through this world will bear some positive effect on others and that I shall have contributed to making the world's moral climate more temperate, more compassionate, more liberating for others. Of course, I shall also bequeath the effects of my selfishness, my pride, and my greed. Human society will inherit the mistakes I made while groping toward a realization of my true identity as a child of God. Many of my mistakes will cause others to stumble or to decide that following Jesus should not cost too high a price. Nevertheless, I do have my hope, and when I understand myself, I see that the basis of this hope lies in the fact that I do not journey through this world alone. Other men and women, more clear-sighted and more steadfast than I, are also traveling through this world and their virtue might compensate for my blindness. Because of their efforts, I can hope that together we shall have made the world more human, more just and patient. Further, I believe that when we are acting and living at our best, we are cooperating with the profound, steady pull of God's grace which inspires people of every time and place to dream the kingdom and to donate their lives and hearts to working for others. I believe that our efforts are best when they coincide with the words and example of Jesus. I may hope, therefore, that God will never abandon us in our struggles or in our vision of the kingdom because God would not allow death to bury the faith and the work of Jesus. In the end, I hope that God will always love me. Jesus gave his life to tell me this.

Jesus, the soul, resurrection. There are so many pages already written about these doctrines that it is probably unnecessary to add anything else. At the same time, these doctrines are so relevant to our experience that the Christian community will always be reflecting on them. These doctrines shape and govern our religiousness; they provide the guidelines within which we explain who we are. My few reflections by no means pretend to be exhaustive. I simply wish to suggest a way of understanding these doctrines which corresponds to personal experience, a way which might serve to channel one's understanding of other beliefs as well. And so the book falls conveniently into three chapters.

In the opportunities I have had to conduct courses for religious educators, candidates for the permanent diaconate, and adult Christians in parishes, as well as for undergraduates at Holy Cross, I have noticed the recurrence and the appeal of the religious concerns addressed here. There is no greater satisfaction a religion teacher can enjoy than helping people to realize something about their faith they did not understand before, and generally this happens when one shows how doctrines arise from and speak to people's experience. This is particularly true when the teacher explains passages of Scripture and shows the relevance of God's word to daily life. The Emmaus story is a good example of what I mean. There Jesus is the teacher who awakens fresh hopes in his disciples when he joins them on their journey and interprets for them their own recent experience in terms of the Scriptures. I should add, however, that I have not been able to elicit much enthusiasm for theoretical religious concerns, such as the development of trinitarian theology, the theology of the real presence of Christ in the Eucharist, or the doctrine of infallibility. Let me explain that Catholics are interested in understanding their sacraments, they believe in the Trinity, and they listen to the Pope. But it has been my experience that Catholics are less interested in aspects of sacramental theology, for example, than in liturgy which is alive and which speaks to them in words that are clear and prayerful, and that illuminate God's presence in their daily living. And when their liturgical expectations are heightened, when they have begun to taste how the breaking open of Scripture nourishes their daily lives, then they will be quite disappointed if their parish liturgies are celebrated dryly and perfunctorily, or if their priest speaks about the Gospel without imparting a sense that he has experienced the Spirit. People should, at least occasionally, be leaving church and saying, "Were not our hearts burning within us while he talked with us . . . and opened the Scriptures to us?" (Luke 24:32).[2]

To take another example, many Catholics do not know the background and technical meaning of papal infallibility. Even after these are explained, papal infallibility continues to float at the periphery of our religious lives, for most Catholics do not bother about theoretical religious issues. Many people are good Christians, after all, without subscribing to the doctrine of papal infallibility. Besides, one suspects that the notion of infallibility has often been enlisted to bolster papal influence and a monarchical view of Church authority. One suspects further that the Catholic's attitude toward the papacy has often been based on an attitude toward authority in general, and that this attitude, at least in the United States, has little to do with the Gospel and a lot to do with political and economic convictions. Many people want civil and religious authority to reaffirm their sense of security. They do not mind a Pope teaching authoritatively about religious beliefs, but they are less likely to listen when he challenges economic policies or the way rich nations wield their economic and military power.

Theologians have pointed out at some length that religious truth needs to be approached in terms of correct action, not merely in terms of correct thinking. They have also insisted that infallibility should not be viewed as a private privilege of the Pope but must be situated within the broader context of the Spirit's presence to the Church. When the Pope witnesses to the risen Jesus by championing the rights of the poor and oppressed, and by working on behalf of justice and disarmament, and when the style of his ministry reminds people of Jesus' promise to dwell among his disciples, then the doctrine of infallibility is subtly redrawn. Essentially, the Catholic realizes, a community comes to know the truth by doing Christian things. If infallibility is to have any relevance to the practice of faith, then the Church's concern for standing in the truth should not be construed as a preoccupation with the correctness of religious dogmas but as a concern for fidelity to evangelical living.

Now that I have oriented the reader to the plan and tone of these pages, I should like to add two further sets of comments by way of introduction. The first is a general point about religious doctrine which I make in order to explain, roughly, why not every doctrine carries the same weight in the unfolding of the life of faith. The second summarizes some lessons to be learned from the history of Christian spirituality. I include them, even though I shall not be discussing each of them in detail, in order to draw attention to the nature and the range of those religious teachings which do bear directly on the actual living out of Christian faith.

A Word about Doctrine

The doctrines of Christian faith are interconnected. If our understanding of original sin changes, for example, then so will our approach to the sacrament of baptism, in terms of both its liturgical celebration and its theology. By interpreting original sin less in private terms and more as social evil, it becomes easier to see that the central liturgical moments of baptism are our being drawn into the community of believers and our being incorporated into the dying and rising of Jesus. Being washed clean of original sin is a negative way of declaring that one is now part of the Church, the redeemed community of men and women who have been shown where evil and alienation exist in human society and who can now, with Christ, create a community where people may lead truly reconciled lives as sisters and brothers.[3] There will also be corresponding adjustments in our understanding of grace, of redemption, of the Church's mission, and of what it means to be human. When the opening chapters of the Book of Genesis came to be read, in our own time, more symbolically than historically, there had to be eventual shifts in the way we read other portions of the Bible, including some (not all) of the miracle stories, the narratives about Jesus' birth and childhood, and certain events in the life of Jesus, such as the temptations in the wilderness and the transfiguration.

Furthermore, an interpretation of a particular doctrine might make greater sense within one historical or theological perspective than another. It made sense during the Middle Ages to interpret Jesus' death in terms of satisfaction and atonement; in feudal society offended honor had to be restored by one in a position to make fair restitution. Dishonor to God, the sovereign of heaven and earth, could only be repaired by one who was equal to God. Thus, only the Son could atone for human sin. Today, for the most part, the medieval perspective holds little meaning for us, although there have been attempts to retrieve its significance.[4] Since our mentality is not feudal, we are less likely to think about sin as an offense against the God whose honor needs to be restored. We do not experience the world as twelfth century people.

Sometimes, in understanding religious teaching, we have to stay alert to shifts of imagery. Older images and metaphors may no longer speak to us, but the meaning beneath them can. Thus, we don't think of demons flying around our rooms, taking the shapes of snakes, tigers, or goblins, which is how demons were depicted by ancient monks like Antony and Pachomius. Even the Gospel accounts of demonic possession are not likely to resonate with the experience of most educated people today. That people should be plagued by doubts, however, tormented by a heart with divided loyalties, burdened by fear or led astray by false values—these are facts most of us understand. The shape of demons may have changed; their haunting fears and seductions have not. The desert or wasteland experience is very much a part of life in the twentieth century.

Sometimes, too, teachings which once mattered a great deal to the Church no longer play a major role in the ordinary living out of faith. Theological reflection has clarified some of the presuppositions behind particular teachings and has shown that those teachings do not occupy a central (nor perhaps even a marginal) connection with the Gospel. The doctrine of limbo and the practice of gaining indulgences are good examples. The belief that those who die without baptism will not be saved is another example.

And then there are doctrines, officially still on-the-books, which arose in the thick of religious or theological controversies but whose significance has receded because the questions and debates which gave rise to those doctrines are no longer pressing or meaningful. The doctrine that Christ has two wills, that he was begotten not made, as the Creed says, and the claim that it is more blessed to remain in virginity or celibacy than to be joined in sacramental marriage, might be examples of this. One might add to this, though not for the sake of calling their legitimacy into question, those doctrines which are subscribed to by Catholics but which do not figure significantly in their daily practice of faith. Such teachings might help to define Catholic identity, but they do not appear to shape the Catholic's consciousness and behavior. The doctrines of the virgin birth, papal infallibility, and purgatory might be instances of teachings which do not exert a transformative effect upon daily Christian living, at least for most believers.[5]

What holds for doctrine also holds for principles and teachings underlying the spiritual life. Certain themes or principles figure significantly into the believer's growth in

faith and holiness, and the major themes are interconnected. In a moment I shall describe some of them. Different periods in the history of Christianity have mani-
fested their own ideals of perfection and holiness.
Basically, Christians everywhere have understood that
holiness consists of loving God and loving their neighbor,
and that the actual living out of the Christian way (as
opposed to simply knowing what Christian faith teaches)
depends upon being led and empowered by the Spirit of
Jesus. Yet there are differences in living out the Gospel.
These differences arise because of the personalities of
individual Christians (like Antony of the Desert, or Bene-
dict, or Francis of Assisi, or Ignatius Loyola), differences
of culture, and differences of history. Leading a contemplative life in the southern United States, for instance, will
be different from leading a contemplative life in northern
Thailand. Working on behalf of the poor in Chicago or
Glasgow will be different from working on behalf of
human rights in Central America. Or again, being an apostle of Jesus Christ meant one thing to St. Paul, something
else to Francis Xavier, and still something else to Christians like Dietrich Bonhoeffer and Dorothy Day.

Christian spirituality cannot help but be influenced
by developments in theology, in philosophy, in psychology, or in social and economic analysis. What theologians
say about grace and freedom sooner or later has an impact
on the way people are instructed in their personal responsibilities, their sense of sin, and their expectations about
God's mercy and judgment. Or again, because of the work
of Karl Marx, the Christian community, in attempting to
discern what the Gospel demands today, must take into
account the way political and economic institutions often
oppress and dehumanize people. Contemporary spirituality necessarily assumes political and social dimensions.

Christians today cannot afford to be uninformed about whose economic interests are being served by their work, by their politics, by their values, or by their financial and social goals. In short, theology is conditioned by time and place, by culture and history, and by personalities and religious assumptions of which a particular age might not be fully aware.

In spirituality, two major adjustments are possible, and they often occur together. Behind the way Christians move toward God are an understanding of what it means to be human and an understanding of what God is like. If one's idea of human nature shifts, there will be corresponding changes in one's view of sin and grace, the relation between contemplation and action, the meaning and purpose of sacraments, what it means to be church, and the nature of that perfection to which Jesus calls us. If one's understanding of God changes (and this generally happens in response to changes in our understanding of the human person as God's image), then there will be corresponding adjustments in the way we hear and interpret Gospel texts, our appreciation of creation, the final destiny of human beings, the place of non-Christian religions in God's redemptive plan, and the way we discern or recognize the Spirit's action in our lives.

The spiritual life is, after all, a way of *life*. It is responsive to stimuli which come from our culture, our family backgrounds, the city or town where we grew up, the vitality of the religious community around us, the scientific outlook of the time, and so on. How else could an historically revealing God become manifest to us except through the circumstances, events, outlook, people, and experiences of our lives? Many Christians have grown up without ever hearing Gregorian chant, or without ever setting eyes on the Pope, or without being able to read Scripture in their own language. Some lived at a time when Church leaders had given scandal because of their material affluence, their intellectual narrowness, and the spiritual diffidence of their lives. Some, like the Protestant reformers, reacted with disappointment which turned to outrage; others, like the French peasants in the eighteenth century who revolted against both Church and throne, reacted with disillusionment that turned to rejection of the Church. Some Christians have grown up when new ideas and discoveries were being generated in philosophy and science, and others when Christian nations had betrayed the cause of peace and brought the world to war. Many a believer during the seventeenth century must have been thrown off balance by the proof that the earth was not the center of the solar system, just as in our own day many were unsettled by the discovery that human beings could control the size of their families by artificial means. Christians living in the first century had been eagerly awaiting the second coming of Jesus, while many of those living at the end of the twentieth century are striving feverishly to eliminate the prospect of a nuclear apocalypse and to remove economic injustice from the face of the earth. One person is favored with visions, another is afflicted with headaches. One person wants to raise children and another is drawn to a life of solitude. One has to carry the burden of psychological problems, another is guilt-ridden or outraged over his government's failure to act justly. Obviously, the variations are almost endless. But I have risked stating what is so obvious in order to draw attention to the historical, human situations in which people have to learn how to hear God, to do their best in following God's call, and to esteem the everyday character of their salvation history.

Doctrines are related. Changes in one require adjusting our understanding of others. Furthermore, doctrines have a bearing on Christian spirituality. In fact, it may prove to be the case that unless doctrines have some bearing on spirituality, then they really are not central to the Gospel and do not deserve a great deal of attention. This is simply another way of stating that truth must relate to life; otherwise, whatever teaching or doctrine we are talking about should not be called a truth. The chapters of this book reflect, then, the bearing of certain ideas on spirituality, an understanding of doctrines which I have found personally thought-provoking. Who is Jesus? What are my hopes? What is it, finally, that is being created in and through human living? To raise any one of these questions is to invite the other two. But I repeat, the chapters are not intended to be final, comprehensive treatments of Jesus, the soul, and the resurrection.

Fifteen Features of Christian Life

The second set of remarks I wish to make at the outset summarizes themes in the history of spirituality. I am mentioning them here because they are not treated in the book, although they are important; besides, they help to sketch the horizon of Christian experience within which my ideas on Jesus, the soul, and resurrection are being presented. From my reading of works in the area of Christian spirituality, I have noticed about fifteen recurrent ideas. Not every writer deals with each idea either directly or indirectly. But from studying a representative number of spiritual works, one would sooner or later uncover the major ideas emerging within the tradition. Again, I list them here, not as a comprehensive summary, but as a lesson in the wisdom and balance of Christian spirituality. In addition, while most of these ideas are not official Church doctrines, I think they all qualify as the living doctrine which arises from Christian experience and which then serves to shape the Christian pattern of existence.

1. *The nature of and the need for spiritual direction.* This point will perhaps sound all too obvious to people who have either given or received spiritual direction, but there are many others who either have never heard about this or who have thought that spiritual direction is reserved to priests, sisters, and the pious faithful. Throughout the tradition, however, Christians have been aware that they need to talk with others who are also praying and trying to follow Christ faithfully. Being a Christian is a way of being together as men and women with shared hope and a common view of life. We have our questions and difficulties about how to pray, to find God, to make the proper decision, to dispose of our surplus goods, to deal with those who make us angry, to live openly and chastely without losing our ability to show affection. Spiritual direction is not only important for dealing with issues like these. It is also one way in which the Spirit shows us how we have to depend upon one another for our growth in holiness. No one arrives at full spiritual insight alone. All of us make mistakes, and without help we run the risk of treading the same spiritual waters for long periods of time. Contemporary interest in spiritual direction arises from a tradition that goes back at least to the desert Christians of the third and fourth centuries. This tradition winds its way through the Middle Ages, the spiritual revival of the sixteenth century with the Carmelites, John of the Cross and Teresa of Avila, and with the Spiri-

tual Exercises of Ignatius Loyola; it continues through people like Francis de Sales and right into our own time.[6]

2. *Personal spiritual experience as the basis of one's coming to know God.* This theme initially surprised me, not for its claim but for its recurrence. It begins with the New Testament period and moves forward, through early Church writers like Irenaeus and Origen, and then into the first monasteries. It was sometimes overlooked and had to be rescued by Christians frequently suspected (and often convicted) of heresy. It is found in the modern Protestant and Catholic revival movements, and features in the renewed efforts at evangelization in today's Church. There were periods when *experience* was regarded as a dangerous word in theology, and that suspicion led to some rather sterile discussions of faith. Some in the Church were nervous about allowing that God could be experienced by ordinary believers apart from exotic-sounding gifts like infused contemplation, inner visions, locutions, and mystical marriages. How many people would have dared to admit to having experienced such things? Today the category of experience has become a major ingredient of theological reflection. We ought never to stop saying, with a bow to Thomas à Kempis, that one is saved not by knowing how to define God but by experiencing God.[7]

3. *The critical importance of discernment.* In the light of the first two ideas, this makes a great deal of sense. If people are going to talk about their hopes, their desires, and their experience, and if they are to trust their experience as that place in which God meets them, then they must also learn how to tell what comes from God and what comes from their fears, their misapprehensions, their fantasies, or from "the demons." Ignatius Loyola distin-

guished good and evil spirits, and he gave a now classical expression to this ancient religious conviction that the movements of the soul need to be discerned if a person is to avoid self-deception, personal harm, and perhaps to avoid leading others into an understanding of God which imprisons rather than liberates the believer.

Ignatius also proposed some guidelines for thinking with the Church. In fact, so had St. Paul. In trying to help the Christians at Corinth discern the Spirit's gifts, Paul instructed them that not every new teaching was consonant with the apostolic tradition, not every gift helped to build up the community, and not every action was guided by the love of Christ. In short, the believing community has its own corporate experience to draw upon. If individuals are not to fall prey to an idiosyncratic interpretation of the mystery of Christ or be led astray by their own enthusiasm, then they should be willing to let the community assist their discernment with its corporate wisdom.

4. *Prayer as the unfolding of one's desire for life.* It is not difficult to define what prayer is so long as one pays attention to what prayer means. Prayer means the whole orientation of the human being toward God, the final "object" of the heart's desire. When individuals become conscious of that desire, in whatever form that awareness takes, then prayer has begun. What is striking is not that throughout the tradition Christians have prayed; that much is presupposed. What strikes me is the insistent prayer of desire for God. People thirst for God, they seek the divine presence, and they do so with such earnestness and love that one cannot help but notice how human beings do not feel complete until they experience themselves united with God, the Lord and giver of life.

While many of us might be content with praying occasionally—thanking God for gifts, asking for favors, expressing sorrow for sin—the people I am describing pray much more basically and simply. They do indeed thank and praise God, they attend the liturgy and read Scripture; but what governs their spiritual life is an intense desire. From desert Christians like Antony to Charles de Foucauld, from *The Cloud of Unknowing* to John of the Cross, from the *Confessions* of Augustine to *The Way of a Pilgrim* or the meditations of Carlo Carretto, the theme is clear. To me it means that the Christian prays with the whole of his or her life. Because of our deep-seated desire for God, we pray with words which might not seem like a prayer (since such praying might not be a matter of words); yet indeed we pray. The things people do, the way they live and act toward others, their spontaneous thoughts and dreams, all of these can be prayers arising from an intense longing for God.

5. *The journey motif.* So much has been written on this that I need only indicate its prominence in the tradition. The journey theme forms a large part of the biblical narrative. From the call of Abraham, the wandering of the Israelites through the wilderness of Sinai, the story of Ruth, the exile in Babylon, to the Markan account of Jesus making his way to Jerusalem and his cross, the journeying of Paul described in the Acts of the Apostles, and the historical journeying of the Church through persecution to glory in the Book of Revelation, the theme has been impressed upon the Christian imagination. In fact, the Islamic tradition, according to the Sufis, tells the story that Adam left the garden and undertook a long historical pilgrimage through time because such wandering would ultimately bring the human race to greater wisdom than it

would have shared had the first human beings never left Eden.[8]

Beyond the biblical narrative there has been the Christian practice of making pilgrimages to holy places. Furthermore, the journey metaphor aids in interpreting one's spiritual experience. I think that the prominence of the theme helps us to see not only that faith has its own kind of geography, but that one cannot come into contact with the living God and expect to remain in the same place for very long. Inwardly or outwardly, there must be a journey.

6. *The nature of Christian religious experience: knowing God as the Father of Jesus Christ.* I cannot state that this idea is as recurrent as I would wish, but it certainly can be located in the New Testament and occasionally afterward. Perhaps this theme will not be set into relief unless the Christian finds himself or herself living in the midst of non-Christians and in a non-Western culture, and then wonders what is peculiar to the Christian's experience of God. Such a situation would force us to make explicit, from our own experience, what was so clearly a part of Jesus' religious experience. God, for Jesus, was "Abba," and this was both a title and an abbreviation for the whole range of Jesus' experience of God.[9] Behind this name there lies Jesus' enormous confidence in God's love for him and for us, a loving trust which helps us to understand how Jesus learned what he was to teach others. Jesus lived and spoke as he did because he experienced God in a particular way.

Christians experience God, but they always experience God in and through Jesus. Knowing God as Jesus did requires, for us, an experience of Jesus, and this is exactly what the Spirit makes possible. That explains why devotion to Jesus remains a central feature of the tradition. We do not simply learn about Jesus and then, having learned about God from him, move on to experience God directly. From age to age, Jesus stays at the center of Christian prayer and living because knowing Jesus gives rise to knowing the God who is his Father and is now our "Abba" too. Even what Julian of Norwich meant by referring to God as mother only makes sense within the context of what "Abba" meant for Jesus. The warmth behind Jesus' teaching and healing reveals a God as much mother as father, as much friend as creator, a God truly his father dearest.

7. *The shifting place of the humanity of Christ in one's relationship with God.* This theme is not the theological problem of relating the divine and human natures, although that certainly has had a bearing on Christian spirituality. Indeed, whenever they concentrate on the divinity of Christ, Christians run the risk of forgetting that Jesus was truly one of us. In his sermons for the feast of the ascension, for instance, St. Augustine explained to his listeners that Jesus' ascending to the Father was for their good because, as long as they could see the human features of Jesus, they would not be drawn to contemplate his divinity. But left unchecked, this sort of contemplation eventually results in our losing the full richness of Christian faith which comes from seeing Jesus as bearing and transforming our humanity. The point here, however, is that some Christians, after years of prayer and meditation, have found that their images of Jesus are inadequate to their experience of him. Like Mary Magdalene, they want to hold on to Jesus, but he resists their efforts to cling to him. In fact, some generations of Christians even try to

protect their picture of Jesus from being painted anew by people of another generation or of a different culture.

The humanity of Jesus is neither incidental nor provisional to the Christian experience of God. We depend upon our images of Jesus to carry us into the Holy Mystery which God is, and every one of those images has to be evaluated in terms of its correspondence with Easter faith. The way in which Jesus is human speaks to us of the Father with whom he is one. But the problem is learning how to allow Jesus to have a transformed humanity without bypassing one's own humanity in the process. We are not yet like the risen Jesus; we cannot afford to undervalue the material world or to suppose that flesh and blood are incidental to genuine religious experience. Nor can we afford to ignore our rootedness in history, the time and place, the political and cultural circumstances out of which we respond to Jesus' call to discipleship. Here I cannot develop a firm and precise account of the place which Christ's humanity actually assumes in our relationship with God. I want merely to indicate that occasionally our familiar picture of Jesus slips away. Some Christians feel guilty when this happens. They blame themselves for having been unfaithful to Jesus (although they are not sure how) and they attempt to recover the form and intimacy of their earlier relationship. Other Christians think that they have outgrown Jesus (although they would be reluctant to say this) and have entered into a direct relationship with the Father, or, simply, with the absolute mystery of God. The tradition cautions two things. First, one cannot retrace an earlier stage of faith. Jesus brings us, just as he led his first followers, to view his humanity and ours in the transfiguring light of the resurrection. This world, human history, the everydayness of life, are never transcended, but they are transfigured. Second, while a person might

conclude that he or she has outgrown Jesus, it is usually
the case that one has come to a more profound and penetrating relationship with God precisely because of Jesus.
In other words, it is Jesus who continues to draw us into
an ever richer experience and understanding of the divine
presence, even when one does not recognize the Jesus
who leads. As one draws closer to God the likelihood of
having to wrestle with difficulties like these increases.[10]

8. *The necessity of undergoing purgation and the
way of the cross.* Many readers are probably acquainted
with the classical spiritual model of the three ways—the
way of purgation, the way of illumination, and the way of
contemplative union. Progress in the spiritual life nor-
mally takes one through these "stages," although, like all
models, this one only approximates actual experience. I
have met some Christians who say, quite humbly, that they
have been enduring purgation their whole life. And yet, as
they describe their experience, they reveal a high degree
of familiarity and union with God.

Nevertheless, the tradition bears witness to the fact
that no one draws close to God without being cleansed or
purged. Sinfulness needs to be identified and acknowl-
edged; the long process of ascesis has to begin. Repen-
tance takes a while because one generally discovers that
sin runs deeper, is more widespread and tenacious, more
serious, than one would have thought as a plain, simple
sinner. Christians do not sin more than anyone else. But
the words of Jesus—"Father, forgive them, for they do not
know what they are doing"—are harder on Jesus' disciples because the disciples are often the ones who do know
what they are doing. The real nature of sin becomes clear,
and the need (as well as the desire) for purgation, for forgiveness, for being made worthy of God's love, grows

insistent. Furthermore, purgation or ascesis affects not only the heart but the mind as well. The mind can quickly fall in love with its own light; it is easily impressed by its own insight and would sew up reality with ideas and images which are narrow and comfortable rather than vigorous and liberating. And so the Spirit teaches the mind how little it truly knows or comprehends. The mind blunders and its ignorance has to be shattered by the foolishness of the cross and the wisdom of God. All this hurts: the mind is humbled and healed by God's grace.

The cross is obviously a central Christian symbol; it lies at the core of Christian experience. It is no surprise that the theme of the cross should be treated extensively and in depth by spiritual writers. But spiritual writers are not concerned with the theological aspects of the cross—the nature of redemption, how the Eucharist continually represents the mystery of Jesus' dying (and rising), and so forth. They are concerned with the way believers continue to experience in their own lives the mystery of Jesus' dying and the encounter of the disciple with the love and forgiveness of the crucified Jesus. The love of Jesus—both his love for us and ours for him—is a purifying love.[11]

9. *"Negative knowledge" of God: the inadequacy of human images and concepts about God.* There is a swift current in the tradition of both Eastern and Western Christianity (though by no means the dominant current) which reminds us that God is always greater than our ways of thinking and describing the divine reality. This is not only to repeat what Thomas Aquinas said about the inevitability of our knowing God only through analogy with created things. (For instance, one affirms that God is good; but no created goodness can compare with divine goodness, and thus on that score God is not good, that is, not good

according to our limited perception of what goodness means. Still, goodness is greater than we are. Goodness is something in which we participate, and God is supremely good with a goodness that surpasses human measures of goodness. Aquinas' technique sounds more cumbersome than it actually is, and he intended only to safeguard the transcendence of God. Aquinas knew that, unlike science, theology could never get a conceptual handle on the mystery it seeks to understand.)

But the negative knowledge of God, as discussed by spiritual writers, refers to the way some believers actually experience the inadequacy of familiar ideas and images describing God. The experience is usually distressing, at least until a person learns that others have gone through the same sort of spiritual emptying and begins to realize that what is happening in his or her life is taking place because the Spirit is present. Sometimes it is difficult for such a person to know the difference between an experience of God as absent and an experience of having one's mind and imagination emptied of familiar categories and ideas. It can prove distressing because the individual may think that he or she has lost faith, when all the while faith is growing deeper, more subtle, and sightless. The soul passes into a kind of "dark night," a "cloud of unknowing," a siege of inner blindness.

I want to stress that this does not appear to be a universal Christian experience by any means. But it is reassuring to know, if one does start to feel plunged into a not-knowing where the line between unbelief and the belief to which one has grown accustomed becomes blurred, that others have passed through similar turmoil of soul. One has not stopped loving God, but the God whom one is loving no longer appears to be "there" in the same way. The proof that faith is actually deepening is that love itself does not waver even though the eye of faith feels blinded. This is one of the strains of Christian mysticism. It is particularly evident in the writings of Gregory of Nyssa, Meister Eckhart, and John of the Cross.[12]

The Carthusian writer, Thomas Verner Moore, distinguished two ways, the Way of Peace and the Way of Patience. He wrote:

> Most devout souls living an interior life walk in the Way of Peace. But from time to time their Way of Peace leads them into the Way of Patience. Few, very few souls, pass their whole life in the Way of Patience; but great will be their reward in eternal life. Peace often illumines the sickroom and the prison cell. But sometimes it does not. Our Lord whispers to the soul: "Be thou faithful unto death and I will give thee the crown of life." And the whisper may give at once patience and fidelity. And so in the slave labor camps of Siberia there seem to be some who are called to live and die in the Way of Patience. And patience hides a hidden peace that makes endurance quite possible. Those who go far in the Way of Peace have already on earth a foretaste of what it means to live with God in eternity. "I to my beloved and His turning is towards me" expresses the habitual union of the soul with God in the Way of Peace. And those who walk, faltering through physical weakness, on the Way of Patience see God also, but dimly and darkly through the tears of sorrow and trial.[13]

The Way of Patience might not sound like John of the Cross' description of the dark night of the soul, but it characterizes rather well, I think, the experience of many believers. They find themselves always waiting on the God they know to be there but who is so silent, and they fear from time to time that the silence of God might be the stillness of death. And yet, while the mind feels so terribly empty and alone, the soul fills with love and compassion for the world. Waiting is a form of suffering, and the fruit of that suffering is a love made more intense because it seems so unreasonable.

10. *The significance of poverty: physical, existential, and spiritual.* Since Jesus told his disciples on various occasions that they must sell what they have and give their money to the poor before following him, we expect to find spiritual writers considering and applying this teaching. And they do, many times over. To be a Christian and to come closer to God requires becoming poor.

Poverty, however, unfolds on several levels. Material poverty seems to be the most dramatic because it is so visible. Francis of Assisi exemplified a rigorous form of physical poverty; other disciples of Jesus throughout the centuries who have wanted to imitate him as closely as possible and to give persuasive witness to the truth of the Gospel have practiced poverty, often in the extreme. The difficulty is that poverty is not a good thing. Poverty cannot be attractive to those who are destitute, not by choice, but through misfortune or economic injustice. For Christians to practice a literal form of poverty makes sense only as a way of expressing solidarity with the poor. Poverty should not be romanticized, which frequently happens when someone talks of the "poor Christ." The Church has waged its own war against material poverty and the tragic signs of poverty—ignorance, disease, hunger, unemployment, crime—by establishing and supporting schools, printing presses, hospitals, clinics, food banks, cottage industries, and so on. The Church has emphatically preached the social implications of the Gospel's call to faith by underlining the requirement of doing justice.

There is another form of poverty, the existential kind. This is not a poverty one chooses to experience but the poverty which characterizes the human being. Each man or woman who thinks about life must come to terms with the ultimate sign of human poverty, namely, death. For death is the word that tells us we can own absolutely nothing, beginning with our very lives. This poverty is experienced by believers, it is described by spiritual writers, and it needs to be understood. Jesus too had to endure this kind of poverty because he was truly human. Otherwise, his solidarity with us would have finished with his being materially poor, and material poverty is not a feature of many Christian lives today. But existential poverty is. Facing up to the fact that we are incapable of being owners (only God can "own" anything), that all our possessions and accomplishments must eventually perish, and that life itself is not ours to keep, can lead to a grim view of reality unless our outlook is relieved by glimpses of God's grace. Existential poverty which is endured without a taste of God's love becomes another feature of human alienation. Death appears as the consequence of sin, the sin of trying to grasp and possess what only God can own.[14]

Spiritual poverty is what the Gospel is talking about. It means detachment, it means stewardship, it means realizing that before God all of us are sisters and brothers and that this relationship must color the way Christians think about economics, politics, and social responsibilities. Spiritual poverty is a view of reality wherein one sees how all things come from God. Or rather, it is the ability to spot grace as grace, to notice the gift-character of life, and to bless God both in good times and in bad. The person who realizes his or her dependence on God, and who lives that truth faithfully and thoroughly, is spiritually poor. This is the only kind of poverty which should be called evangelical, for without it existential poverty can lead to a cold despair and material poverty can lead to hardness of heart. To see what spiritual poverty means the disciple has to meditate on the life of Jesus. The fruit of that poverty which is embraced for the sake of the Gospel is freedom. The text about selling one's goods and giving to the poor is not a recipe for helping the poor. Rather, the text is insisting that one cannot be with Jesus where Jesus wants to be unless one is inwardly free, and the experience of being free confirms that the reign of God has begun.

11. *The place of the mind and the place of the heart in one's spiritual growth.* A number of spiritual writers have warned of the danger of getting lost in one's head and never really learning how to be in God's presence, quietly and effortlessly. True enough, we cannot trade for long on spiritual ideas, no matter how exciting or consoling they seem at first. If the spiritual life is allowed to become a matter of ideas, then prayer will become more and more of a monologue and we will end up talking into empty space. But no purpose is served if mind and heart are juxtaposed, with the intimation that the heart is an ally and the mind is an obstacle to finding God. The mind too has a way of praying. Wisdom and understanding are, after all, gifts of the Spirit. Piety without prudence, spiritual practice without intelligence, can hinder and even harm one's coming closer to God.

Mind and heart are not neatly balanced in terms of truth and love, for the mind loves and the heart reasons. People have to learn, therefore, how to allow both dimensions of the human spirit to reach toward God. This theme might not be so explicitly treated as the others, except in terms of a warning against, on the one hand, intellectualizing one's relationship to God or, on the other hand, substituting zeal for prudence. For me, this theme is important as a lesson to be drawn from the history of spirituality. There have been aberrations and oversights in the tradition, some of which came from ignoring the advice of the past, or from failures to discern the Spirit's action, or from stubborn refusal to listen to the experience of other believers. Jansenism, for instance, may have promoted a well-intentioned form of piety, but it was mistakenly severe. To take another example, the Church was to some degree responsible for the rupture of Christianity in the sixteenth century because it failed to listen to voices calling for religious reform. The Protestant Reformation represented a crisis of spirituality; there was a growing thirst for God and a breakdown in the effectiveness of official carriers of religious experience, such as liturgy and preaching. Examples could be multiplied in the case of individual Christians who launch themselves enthusiastically into religious waters but who have no use for theologians, or in the case of institutional Christians who reject the charismatic renewal out of hand as emotional and unstructured, or in the case of communities which want to lead radically evangelical lives without taking into consideration their obligations toward those in their midst who are not yet so fully committed to spiritual perfection.

12. *The experience of grace as personal and corporate reality.* The previous idea leads into this one. The grace of Christ is personal, not private. We are given the Spirit, though not as a private endowment. The Spirit resides in individual Christians for the sake of drawing them together. The grace of Christ moves people to form

church, to be a fellowship of believers or a community of disciples. The recurrence of this theme, which is particularly Catholic, is remarkable. There is a story in the Life of Pachomius about a monk's dream. In it he sees a line of the brethren, each blind, making his way through perilous places by holding onto the brother in front of him while the leader dimly sees the way to safety. The dream illustrates how some early Christians experienced their dependence upon one another. In her autobiography, Dorothy Day tells how much her being drawn to the Church was an attraction to community. Her sense of that community was not the active exchange among believers we are accustomed to look for today. It was pre-Vatican II, as it were, a view of community which was more formal and spiritual. Yet it was inner communion with others throughout the world which drew her toward the Catholic Church. She wrote:

> I had heard many say that they wanted to worship God, in their own way and did not need a Church in which to praise Him, nor a body of people with whom to associate themselves. But I did not agree to this. My very experience as a radical, my whole make-up, led me to want to associate myself with others, with the masses, in loving and praising God. Without even looking into the claims of the Catholic Church, I was willing to admit that for me she was the one true Church. She had come down through the centuries since the time of Peter, and far from being dead, she claimed and held the allegiance of the masses of people in all cities where I had lived. They poured in and out of her doors on Sundays and holy days, for novenas and missions. . . . They accepted the Church. It may have been an unthinking, unquestioning faith, and yet the chance certainly came, again and again, ''Do I pre-

fer the Church to my own will," even if it was only
the small matter of sitting at home on Sunday morning
with the papers? And the choice was the Church.[15]

To be a Christian is to open oneself to the possibility
of being drawn into companionship with others, to
depend on them for understanding and acceptance, for
sharing faith. God draws men and women together, and
together they are drawn into union with God.

13. *Devotion to Scripture and to the Eucharist.*
Again, the prominence of word and sacrament is hardly
surprising, for they are the two privileged places in which
Christians have come to meet Jesus in their prayer.
Whether reading Scripture slowly and meditatively, interpreting portions of the Bible for others, preaching the
word, or excerpting brief verses which can be repeated
over and over as expressions of what one has always
wanted to say to God, Christians have prized Scripture as
a great treasure. In every age, the Church is renewed when
the Gospel is preached in such a way that people grasp its
meaning afresh, when they leave the liturgy with their
minds quickened by a new experience of the word of God.

If Scripture is the word on which believers feed, their
bread of life, then their other bread is the Eucharist. All
through the tradition, the Eucharist has occupied center
stage of the Church's life. Sometimes Eucharist refers to
the whole of the Church's worship, its liturgical acknowl-
edgement of God's love for us in Christ. At other times it
refers only to the sacrament. Yet whether designating the
whole of Christian life and worship or the sacrament kept
in a tabernacle to be received and adored, Catholic Christians have perceived here the real presence of Christ in a
pre-eminent way. The catechetical instructions of early

Church writers, the medieval hymns of Thomas Aquinas, the processions, the silent adoration of a Charles de Foucauld in his desert pilgrimage, the sacrament's steady calling upon believers to recognize other Christians as their brothers and sisters, the experience of union with Christ and communion with others throughout the world—these are some of the moments in the unfolding of eucharistic spirituality wherein Jesus is known to be truly present among his disciples.

Scripture and Eucharist are not private elements of individual piety, however. They are not just spiritual means for the individual's growth in holiness. Scripture and Eucharist build the Church, and where Scripture and Eucharist figure intimately into the Church's life, there we find the Christian experiencing what it is to be a community of grace. And so, whether the context is a monastery, a village church or a large urban parish, a family, a charismatic community or a base Christian community, people are discovering why Jesus gave his life. Jesus died so that all might become one: "I in them, you in me, that they may be perfectly one in us." Experiencing ourselves becoming one is to know that the Spirit of Jesus truly resides among us.

The significance of this point will be missed by those who do not understand that the Eucharist is a sacrament of *communion*. Many Christians claim that they want to be joined with Christ, but what they seem to mean is that they want Christ to be joined to them. They expect that the movement of grace will be from Christ's side toward them rather than from their side toward Christ. "Jesus Christ" might serve as another name for union, and so if we really do desire Christ, then our sense of union—our longing for communion with others, our pain at any breakdown in mutual understanding and acceptance, our awareness of really belonging to one another, our gratitude for the communion we already enjoy—is necessarily going to grow.

14. *Prophecy and witness: learning to live with and under the word of God.* People may be driven by their desire for God to adopt exaggeratedly religious lifestyles. They have fled to mountains and deserts, they have spent their lives on top of pillars, they have given away decent clothes and worn rags, they have nearly crippled themselves with fasting and other penances, they have courted martyrdom, all in the name of religion. However sincere, such behavior does not strike me as admirable or as particularly Christian, although I think I understand what would prompt men and women to do such things.

But there is a prompting of the Spirit which brings people to recognize what the word of God is asking of them here and now. They hear it so consistently and strongly that they almost have no choice except to respond. Finding a suitable form for that response can take time, and they might do some strange things before arriving at the concrete decision, work, or lifestyle to which God is drawing them. The theme I am identifying is simply the importance of Christian witness. Sometimes it is the dramatic witness of one confronting religious or political abuse, or the one who forfeits freedom to ransom a slave, or the one who devotes his or her life to working among the poor and diseased, to bring the Gospel to other nations and cultures, to fight on behalf of justice. Imprisonment, ridicule, and isolation often accompany such witness: a witness that convicts society, Church, or political regime of its blindness, a witness that demonstrates how the passion of Jesus is still taking place in the world.

At other times it may be the steady, patient witness of those attempting to live the Gospel as carefully and completely as possible. They do so, not because they want to please their family and friends, nor because they were simply raised in a religious tradition which they never questioned, nor because they are secretly afraid of God and need to feel that they are on God's side. They live the Gospel because they love Christ, and though they might not be able to explain why, they could not imagine living without him.

15. *The discovery that God speaks across religious differences.* This idea is of more recent vintage in Christian spirituality, but it does have ancient roots. Peter appears to have made this discovery when he visited Cornelius' house. "I now realize how true it is that God does not show favoritism but accepts men from every nation who fear him and do what is right" (Acts 10:34–35). Some of the early Christian writers knew that God had spoken through the cultures of the non-Jews. Once the Roman Empire had become Christian, however, the Church was no longer sensitive to the fact that God was larger than Christendom. From time to time, missionaries would realize that non-Christian religion did not mean paganism, and that to die without baptism did not mean automatic deprivation of grace and glory. Today Christians are far more likely to appreciate that God's saving outreach to the world has a larger grasp than we ever imagined. While theologians have offered explanations of how all grace comes through Christ even though most people have never heard the Gospel, it is at the level of spirituality that the reality of God's mystery comes home.

The fear which haunts many Christians is that, if God is present among non-Christians, leading them toward faith and love, then Christian missionary efforts will seem to have been unnecessary and, in fact, Jesus will have been relativized. How would this correspond with our belief in his divinity?

Still, some Christians who have lived surrounded by another religious tradition have sensed a communion at a deeper than creedal level. Non-Christians have spiritual experiences. They grow in holiness, they understand the difference between virtue and vice, they meditate and pray, they learn how to love their neighbor, they give alms to the poor, they know the rhythm of living and dying. With this in mind, there is no reason for Christians to doubt that the God who has brought the human race this far in its religious pilgrimage will abandon men and women who are sincerely seeking to understand how to be faithful to Jesus in a religiously pluralistic world.

Perhaps many Christians never paused to reflect that if Catholics and Protestants were both loving Christ, saying the Lord's Prayer, reading the Gospels and making pilgrimages to the Holy Land, if they were both mindful of the demands of charity toward the poor, and so on, then no matter what divided them, they already shared a considerable degree of communion. For there is only one Spirit, and no one can say that Jesus is Lord except through that Spirit (cf. 1 Corinthians 12:3). Why, therefore, as we grow in our realization that we have been looking at other Christians with blinders on for several centuries, and that we have only widened our mutual distrust and misunderstanding by not speaking to one another, can we not see that perhaps we have yet to learn how many brothers and sisters we really have?

At any rate, this idea has been receiving much attention in recent years. For instance, John S. Dunne writes of "passing over" from one's own religious tradition to another religion, and back.[16] The path Dunne describes is a way of growing in self-understanding and of appreciating the God who speaks across religious differences. The idea also appears in spiritual writers like Thomas Merton and Bede Griffiths, and in theological writers like Karl Rahner and Raimundo Panikkar. I would wager that by the next century many Christians will be drawn to explore and participate in forms of ecumenical spirituality. The Christian community at Taizé in France and the presence of a Hindu-Christian ashram in India may be hints of such development.[17]

We have said enough about the fifteen themes or traits of Christian spirituality. The teachings which I have summarized are living doctrines for several reasons. First, they arise out of the experience of believers who have followed Jesus; the concerns of those people have been practical, not speculative or abstract. And second, when put into practice, these teachings transform men and women so that they become people of God.

What does it mean to be human? To be human is to desire God and to let one's life be guided by that desire. To be human is to follow Jesus. To be human is to be with other men and women who have experienced the same longing and the same attraction to Jesus.

What does it mean to be Christian? To be Christian is to be poor, that is, to live a simple, uncluttered lifestyle. To be Christian is to seek the company of brothers and sisters who follow Jesus and with whom one can talk and pray about life in the Spirit. To be Christian is to proclaim the real presence of Jesus in Scripture and sacrament. To be Christian is to know Jesus and to experience God who is "Abba" to him and to us. To be Christian is to take up a lifelong struggle against the evil which wants to reign over our hearts and minds.

What does it mean to be a person of God? To be a person of God is to be open to God's concerns and to let the word of God rule our loyalties and our decisions. To be a person of God is to praise God with all one's mind as well as with one's heart, for both mind and heart have their ways of praying. To be a person of God is to anticipate and to respect the word of God which arises outside one's own religious circle. To be a person of God is to realize that mind and heart may have to pass through that purifying darkness which is the very mystery of God. To be a person of God is to be a pilgrim in this world.

These are the principal doctrines, I think, of the Christian's religious life. We can express things more simply still. Karl Rahner wrote: "Christian Faith says nothing more than that we have been called into the immediacy of God himself and that this mystery gives itself to us in unspeakable nearness."[18]

1

The Changing Face of Jesus

He had no beauty or majesty to attract us to him, nothing in his appearance that we should desire him. He was despised and rejected by men, a man of sorrows, and familiar with suffering (Isaiah 53:2–3).

As he was praying, the appearance of his face changed, and his clothes became as bright as a flash of lightning (Luke 9:29).

And being in anguish, he prayed more earnestly, and his sweat was like drops of blood falling to the ground (Luke 22:44).

The Son is the radiance of God's glory and the exact representation of his being, sustaining all things by his powerful word (Hebrews 1:3).

Every age has its own way of looking for God, its own style of asking questions and speaking about God, and a particular way of expressing its faith. The third and fourth centuries of Christian history were marked by large numbers of believers withdrawing to deserts and barren places so that no created thing would distract them from their search for God. In the twelfth through the fourteenth cen-

41

turies, many Christians sought refuge from the world within monastic communities in order to find God in contemplative silence. In the modern age, some Christians have worked tirelessly among the poor in the world's slums—perhaps a modern equivalent of the desert wilderness—in the hope of discovering and spreading God's kingdom on earth.

For each period there is a way of doing theology, that is, a manner of thinking, preaching, and writing about God, which illuminates the fundamentally graced inspiration that draws believers at one time to solitude, at another time to social involvement, at still another time toward some combination of activity and prayer. Theological reflection by Christians living within monasteries is likely to sound ascetical and contemplative. Theology which is being done from an inner city might sound apostolic and socially conscious. When theology is done in the context of research libraries and universities, it will sound critical, probing, or courageously speculative. And when theology is being done by people who are neither prayerful nor poor, its tone might sound timid and spiritually impoverished.

The tone of theology also depends on the time and place in which the Church finds itself. The concerns of one age center on interpreting and preaching Scripture. The concerns of another age center on meeting the challenges posed by developments in biology, astronomy, or history. Sometimes the Church has to respond to objections against religion from agnostics and social revolutionaries, while at other times it must face critical problems raised by psychology or philosophy. The Church in our day is confronted by a variety of challenges. Christian theology today must be politically and economically informed; it faces the task of evaluating political and economic policies in the light of the Gospel. Theology has to be in dialogue with historians and psychologists, and it needs to prepare itself for a closer encounter with the world religions. And people still want to know what it means to be fully human; they long for solitude, but they also want to experience genuine human community. Thus theology in our day has served the Church with a rich and varied contribution. Theologians have reflected on the meaning of Scripture; they have engaged in dialogue with the natural and behavioral sciences; they have explored the riches of the Christian tradition; they have written on liturgy, spirituality, and social issues. And they have made intelligent presentations of Christian faith to the modern world which incorporate the idioms and insights of the twentieth century.

Corresponding to each time, place, and situation in which Christians live there seems to be a picture of Jesus. At one time Jesus is the God-centered person who spends time in the desert and solitary places, praying to the Father and waging war against demons. At another time Jesus is the one who heals, forgives, and consoles. Or Jesus is the prophet who denounces hypocrisy, injustice, and false religious worship; he is the preacher who proclaims and teaches the good news about the reign of God. Or Jesus is the great high priest, mediating divine mercy and grace to a broken world, the one who represents the human race before God. For some Christians, Jesus is the good Samaritan, caring for the poor strangers who have been victimized by the world's robbers. For others, he is the redeemer who offers his life to ransom captives. Or Jesus is the victorious king, reigning sovereignly over all creation. Or he is the all-knowing Lord who stands firmly and brightly ahead of his disciples. Or he is the Christ, the Word of God made flesh, the metaphysical cornerstone underlying

every human effort to know the truth, to understand the
world, and to reach genuine self-knowledge. Or Jesus is
the friend, the true self, the faithful and loving companion
along our life's journey.

The theological outlook and spirituality of each generation of Christians take shape in terms of the social problems, the culture, and the political and economic aspirations of their particular time and place. There are other
factors, too, such as new scientific discoveries, philosophy, historical consciousness, and sensitivity to other cultures, which contribute to the form and content of Christian theology and spirituality. Furthermore, individual
believers will, at various periods of their lives, raise particular questions, grow aware of specific religious needs,
and settle upon more or less satisfying ways of relating to
God and talking about spiritual things. The religious pitch
of a person's life, the ideas one has come to adopt about
God and Jesus, and the unique way each of us comes to
worship and speak to God, are the product of innumerable
influences and experiences which every believer under-
goes in the course of a lifetime. Some grow up on farms or
in small towns; others are raised in cities and industrial-
ized societies. Some families exhibit great warmth and
tenderness toward one another; others break apart in
divorce. Some people have physical ailments, some suffer
fits of depression, some are always even-tempered and
good-natured. Each of us has his or her own problems,
questions, small discoveries, permanent uncertainties,
moments of conversion, memories, and hopes. Each has
his or her personal experience of God's absence and
presence.

What are a few of those problems? There are the general challenges we encounter which are part of our religious and psychological development. Each of us learns

that God exercises no magical control over the world, nor does God exact punishment for sin to the third and fourth generations, despite what the Book of Exodus says. We come to learn that God is not like any human parent, that God harbors no grudges, that God is not responsible for our feelings of guilt and inadequacy. God, we must learn, is always on the side of genuine freedom, for human beings thrive religiously and humanly, not in an atmosphere of precept and fear, but in a climate of freedom and love. God is the one from whom all human parenting takes its name.

Other problems are more particular and personal. Each of us will have questions about what is truly necessary for leading an adequately full human life. We may have grown disenchanted with institutional religion and have realized that much of what we once judged terribly important for being Catholic has turned out to be frightfully marginal to our experience of God and our spiritual needs. Or we may be perplexed by the fact that we have little taste for large portions of the Old Testament. We may be unsettled by the fact that we experience Christ in spite of our local parish rather than through it. We may feel guilty and less Catholic because a particular doctrine or moral teaching of the Church has become irrelevant to our practice of faith. Today we don't flee to deserts and monasteries, although we crave solitude. We want to alleviate poverty and hunger, but, given the proportions of the world's needs, we are tempted to surrender even before we begin.

Some problems arise because what we have believed may have been incorrect, misguided, or misunderstood. For example, some Christians believed, incorrectly, that Jesus knew and could have done absolutely everything God knows and does. Whether or not they realize it, such people have made the Gospel of John the normative expression of Catholic faith. To do this is a mistake, for taken by itself the Fourth Gospel leads to a theological exaggeration of Jesus' features. Other Christians refrained from receiving the Eucharist frequently because they knew themselves to be unworthy. They were misguided. Unworthiness is not a sufficient reason for not approaching Jesus. Still other Christians have resented the Church's speaking out on political and social issues because they believe that the kingdom of God is not supposed to be of this world. They have misunderstood the Gospel's meaning.

It is not surprising, therefore, that individual Christians may have somewhat different images of Jesus and that they have been relating to Jesus through their private picture of him. If I find myself to some degree alienated from the Church, then the Jesus I meet in the New Testament may be a figure at the fringe of institutional life, the one who opposes religious authority and hollow worship. Or Jesus could be the one who enjoys the company of plain, simple, sinful yet hardworking people like me. Or Jesus could appear as the one who journeys and has no place to lay his head. Or Jesus could be the one who confronts people—the disciples for their slowness to understand, the crowds for their lack of faith and their preoccupation with acquiring and possessing material things, the religious leaders because of their lust for honor and power. Judging from Mark 6:1–6, Jesus may even have confronted his own family for their unbelief.

I think the point is clear. Many of us tend to favor a particular image of Jesus, or we lean toward a certain Gospel story or set of scriptural texts, which suits our needs, our outlook, or our expectations of God and ourselves. And that image can change. But we should recognize that the person of Jesus is usually accommodated to perspectives that are merely more or less adequate to the lines of grace which are slowly forcing their way to the surface of our lives.

From attending lectures on the Bible and reading up-to-date Scripture commentaries, Christians have had occasion to learn about the considerable amount of pluralism which exists in the New Testament. While there is a basic unity of faith to be found in the assorted writings which comprise the New Testament, there are also various ways of expressing that faith and there are even different (and sometimes, from our point of view, contrasting) doctrinal positions. Each evangelist drew a distinctive portrait of Jesus. By its inclusion with the others, each portrait tells us that no picture of Jesus will ever be complete since no picture of him does full justice to the person it represents. Yet this also tells us that, because of the limitations of his own faith, ideas, and outlook, not even an inspired writer was able to perceive the whole mystery of Christ. What could be interesting to the student of the New Testament is why each picture of Jesus assumed the shape it did. What could be of interest to the student of theology is whether there might be other images of Jesus, not found in the New Testament, which would also put believers in touch with the mystery of their faith.

There is a further issue, however, beyond the matter of theological pluralism, and this issue should keep us vigilant. It is always possible for an image of Jesus to conceal rather than to reveal the presence of God. How did it happen, for instance, that while European missionaries in the sixteenth and seventeenth centuries worked feverishly among the enslaved Indians of South America, the occupying armies and the Christian kings who sent them had fashioned a very different image of Jesus? How did it happen that, while some German Christians because of their opposition to Hitler followed Jesus to prison and death during the Second World War, others were praying to God at the same time and place and contributed to the deaths of millions? How is it that Christians in Northern Ireland terrorize their own people, that some Christian teachers and leaders have intimidated and undermined the efforts of dedicated Christian writers, other teachers, reformers, and social workers? Why is it that God-fearing Christians cannot live on the same soil with God-fearing Muslims, that a white Christian aristocracy in South Africa oppresses black Christians, or that the Christian military in Chile or Brazil could arrest and torture their fellow Christians, lay-people and pastors alike? How can it be that one arch-bishop is killed for speaking on behalf of his oppressed people, while another prelate christens the children of those who murdered the poor? How is it that Christians who have achieved the highest place in American corporations could refuse to acknowledge the injustices caused by the investment practices of their companies in third world countries?

One cannot answer hard questions like these by appealing to the inevitability of a theological pluralism which originates with the charter documents of Christianity, namely, the Gospels themselves. These questions do not suggest a unity of faith within different ways of expressing that faith. Spiritual oversight which leads to sin cannot be blamed on theological pluralism. Unless we are very careful to look for Jesus each day, and to look for him both as a believing community and in the world at large, then we shall certainly be following an image of Jesus at once lifeless and crippling. "You cannot serve both God and money" means we cannot love God and something else on equal terms. What does the Christian spend most of his or her time thinking about, planning for, desiring, working after? What is it that really commands our attention and respect? How do we live, whose opinions do we trust? Whose interests are served by our labor or by our investments? What do we fear, what do we ignore? What kind of material goods do we own, and why did we buy them? Who has enticed us into wanting and purchasing them? What are our political views? Do we care how our local bank makes its money? By responding to questions like these, we can in fact draw the image of our god. There are many Christians whose faith has been eroded by all the concerns Jesus warned against. In fact, they have ceased being disciples. Their faith is no more secure than a sand castle at low tide.

There are reasons, therefore, which explain why a particular image of Jesus emerges. Some of those reasons are cultural, social, or historical; others are political, economic, or psychological. There are public pictures of Jesus which are associated with a given age, and there are the personal and private images which each believer constructs in his or her religious life. Many factors affect the content and style of Christian theology and spirituality. There is no doubt that theological pluralism has always existed in the Church, and rightfully so. Pluralism refers to the fact that there are different ways of stating the same thing, or that various Christian communities have emphasized different aspects of the Gospel message, or that there are different yet evangelically faithful ways of following Jesus. But not every difference among Christians should be ascribed to theological pluralism. When political and economic values refuse to submit to the scrutiny of the Gospel, or when individuals slide into self-centering lifestyles, then the reality of Jesus will suffer distortion. Consequently, our image of Jesus stands in need of continual examination and discernment. The reasons why we are attracted to one or other Gospel text can shed light on how the Lord might be leading us, but it might also reveal a habit of turning away from scenes or lessons which annoy us, which challenge or confuse us, maybe which even threaten us. In the following pages I should like to propose one way of examining what the reality of Jesus means for us, and in doing this I shall offer seven points for reflection.

1. A Little Question of Loyalty

I do not know who first made this observation, but it has occurred to me on numerous occasions that we often take a position on an issue, not so much on the basis of the merits of the case, but on the basis of our loyalty to some teacher or friend, to our profession or social class, to our country or culture. We tolerate or overlook the attitudes and behavior of close friends, while we can be quick to criticize strangers and people we do not like for the very same opinions and behavior. A great deal of our reasoning and arguing may amount to little more than strategies to defend our loyalties. For the most part, we prefer to leave these loyalties unexamined since they cannot be studied without risk. We might just discover that some of our firmest convictions are based on a number of shallow, erroneous, even unchristian attitudes and choices. The process of changing loyalties can be humbling and painful, but that of course is what conversion is all about. Jesus' call for conversion was not a matter of acquiring new ideas, new ethical guidelines, or new information about God. To convert is to have one's heart changed, to fall in love with God in a radically different way. Jesus did not get into trouble because he was teaching catechism to children, or instructing grown-ups to pray the Our Father, or because his disciples had plucked grain on the sabbath. Jesus threatened people because he reminded them that they owed their highest allegiance to God. Many of the Jews were more loyal to the temple, their traditions, or their religious leaders than they were to God; both politically and religiously, people like Pilate and Herod belonged to the Roman emperor. Loyalties like these would have to be challenged and overturned.

Sometimes people find themselves blocked from such change because they do not like the company Jesus keeps. But the fundamental law of discipleship is this: being-with-Jesus means learning to be where Jesus is. Being-with-Jesus should eventually bring us to identify with the world and the people with whom Jesus identifies himself. This sounds like a rather simple point to grasp; it is not so easy to allow such being-with-Jesus to happen, however. Because many of us are accustomed to a private relationship with Jesus as "my friend," "my companion," or "my Lord," we may have to strain to see Jesus moving into the circles of the poor and afflicted, not the poor of the first century, but the poor and oppressed of our time. It is not difficult to read the Gospels and imagine Jesus walking in Galilee or Jerusalem. But it requires considerable imagination and effort to watch where Jesus walks in the world of today. Jesus characteristically wants to be among sinners, among lonely and marginalized people, in the company of those who need a teacher or a physician.

Imagine yourself for a moment walking with Jesus. You've been looking forward to retreating for a few days with him in a quiet place apart from others, maybe on a hillside or by the shore of a lake. Just as you begin talking, Jesus spots a group of children playing by the roadside, and he wants to join them for a few minutes. You go along, somewhat reluctantly. A bit later you are walking again, and this time he sees some men gathering at a tavern. Already you know what is on Jesus' mind, and you stall on the road, resentful that he is not paying you the attention you wanted. Jesus asks, "Do you want to wait in the middle of the road, or will you join me in the tavern?" Again, later on, you're walking through the city and Jesus notices a soup kitchen, or a half-way house for prisoners, or some street people, and by this time you can predict that he is going to break into conversation with them. It seems impossible to be alone with Jesus. Whenever you appear to be on the way toward developing an individual relationship with him, you discover that he is drawing you into the company of other men and women, especially people who are what the Gospels call "sinners."

This is only an exercise of imagination, but it can help to explain why many Christians fail to understand what salvation, and thus the whole mission of Jesus, is all about. Because they envision salvation as being closeted with God for eternity, they assess salvation much too privately. Salvation, for them, is only a personal reward for the faithful believer. But Jesus was ever concerned about people, about his fellow Israelites, about the tax collectors and sinners, about those who had not yet heard his message and who would come to believe in him through the preaching of his disciples. It should never be surprising, then, to find a Christian encountering difficulties in prayer precisely at the point where a private Jesus seems to be breaking away. For we then need to decide whether to join Jesus or to be left standing along the roadside, or, what is worse, to be left holding the hand of a hollow statue of Jesus to which we speak but from which we never hear anything. Christian salvation has to include, therefore, our being rescued from isolation and privacy, from standing alone at the roadside and talking to a lifeless image of Jesus. Being-with-Jesus, being in his company, sets us free to form new loyalties; it intensifies our longing for real communion with other men and women. Jesus both inspires us to love selflessly, to throw in our lot with the people God loves, and to work on behalf of genuine solidarity. Jesus becomes the source and the sign of the union we are seeking. Being-with-Jesus means that we have said yes to God's concerns, and this is the only loyalty a disciple is entitled to have.

2. Jesus as the One Who Transforms Human Hope

There are aspects of organized religion which many believers today find troublesome. They might be bothered by the concentration of ecclesiastical authority in the hands of a small number of male clerics, or they wonder about the irrelevance of certain teachings to the daily practice of their faith. Perhaps they have been offended by a rising tide of religious and political conservatism among Western Christians, or they might be exasperated by a narrow, parochial religious vision among many Catholics.

There is no doubt that as a Church we have made, and continue to make, many mistakes. But we can adjust to living with a faulted Church because each of us has to reckon with living with a faulted self. Indeed, sometimes the Church's light flickers like a candle trying to hold its own against the wind. Yet the Church, that is, the community of people on whose faith and example each of us depends, remains the place where God's presence to the world is recalled, proclaimed, and brought into sharper focus. The divine presence is recalled whenever the scriptural word is read and preached with faith. It is proclaimed whenever the word of faith spoken over bread and wine enables

Jesus to be sacramentally present among his disciples. It is brought into clearer focus whenever the Christian community moves in the world as living evidence that God does indeed reign in some human hearts.

But the sinfulness and mistakes of the Church should not distract us from being religious people. Rather than surrendering to anger and disappointment, the disciple can return to Jesus and ask, "Why then do I continue to follow you?" And the honest answer is that Jesus arouses our hope. He leads us to believe that God desperately loves the human race, and on the basis of that belief our expectations of God have been heightened.

Many of our hopes, it seems to me, have been too individualistic, too private. We overestimate the need for personal accomplishment, the need that says I must leave my mark on the world by contributing something special and memorable for others, for the human race perhaps, or for the kingdom of God. The Christian will indeed leave a mark, but only after learning the lesson that he or she is not Jesus. We are not messiahs or workers of miracles; we are ordinary flesh and blood whom God has called to know Jesus. If we teach, we ought not encourage our students to follow and imitate us, for Jesus is the only one who can rightly be their teacher. If we are parents, we should not seek to fashion our children to our image and likeness, for only God can be truly mother and father to them, and it is Christ's likeness they must carry. If we are ministers of the Gospel, we are not to think that by obeying our words people will be saved. Or if we heal, we should not think that by our power bodies and minds are made whole. For obedience belongs to God, and God alone has the power to make people well. Whatever we accomplish during our lifetimes begins with that personal conversion which allows God to rescue us, daily, from being torn apart by too much good will, too much confidence in our own efforts, too high an estimate of our importance to God's work. In other words, personal hope has to be defined in terms of what we hope God will do for the world through Christ.

Hope must become communal. If the course of history is to remain directed toward Christ, then others will have to pick up where we leave off on the human race's spiritual journey. Others will take our places in the Church and in society and proclaim for their day the word of faith which interprets all things in the light of Christ. They will recall the presence of God that has accompanied human beings thus far on their historical pilgrimage. They will focus for their age the kingdom of God present in their midst. Personal hope cannot afford to be either individualistic or private; it is not a matter of what *I* want from God but what *we* want. Yet how does hope become transformed and enlarged? How does hope become communal and public?

I cannot insist too strongly that hope is transformed through being-with-Jesus where he chooses to be. Jesus creates the possibility for a realized solidarity with the wider world. My private world has to be cracked open, enlarged, and reshaped by the hopes and dreams, the anxieties and fears of other men and women. Such a re-created vision of the world results in nothing less than appreciating the human race from God's point of view. No one can provide a painless formula for bringing about this change. This growth, like creation itself, is God's work. It may hurt, for the Spirit is laboring over the stiff material of our self-centered hearts and narrow minds, preparing them for the new shape or form which will be Christ in us.

3. A Way in Which Jesus Is Not Divine

In the last ten years or so, a great number of books have been written about Jesus. For the most part, these works represent the attempt by theologians to ensure that the modern Church's understanding of Jesus is based on the soundest biblical and historical scholarship. Each book reflects some of the background and cultural concerns of its author. You find, for instance, that the message and mission of Jesus are interpreted from within situations of widespread economic injustice and military repression in Latin America,[1] or from within situations of a religiously pluralistic society, as in Asia,[2] or from the situation of humanity's search for meaning and the Church's gradual loss of prestige, as in Europe. The central theme of Latin American theology is liberation. In the theology of Karl Rahner and Hans Urs von Balthasar the central theme is the incarnation.[3] For Hans Küng, Jesus is the eminently human being who decisively answers humanistic and atheistic rejections of the reality and seriousness of God's involvement in our history.[4] Monika Hellwig presents Jesus as "the compassion of God,"[5] and Sebastian Moore regards Jesus as "the true self."[6] Some writers emphasize the importance of the resurrection as the starting point for reflecting on the meaning and person of Jesus.[7] Others tend to concentrate on Jesus' public ministry, especially his manner of setting people free by healing them, teaching them, and forgiving their sins.[8] In sorting out the Christological contributions of various theologians, one might even speak of "models of Jesus"[9] (and each believer's model of Jesus, I might add, corresponds to a particular view of the Church and of ministry). Jesus has been interpreted within the framework of process philosophy, which develops the philosophical insights of the twentieth century thinker Alfred North Whitehead,[10] from a Marxist perspective,[11] and from within the thought-world of another twentieth century philosopher, Martin Heidegger.[12] Some writers deal with the image of Jesus conveyed in one or other of the Gospels, such as the Jesus of Mark[13] or the Jesus of John.[14]

Furthermore, theologians have attended to the way Christians worship God in liturgy and in personal prayer in order to uncover another rich source of Christological reflection.[15] And there have been studies on the relation between Jesus and the Spirit, since it is through the Spirit that Jesus remains present and active in his community.[16]

All this wealth of writing on the person of Jesus has certainly illumined our understanding of the faith. Christians need not be timid about their belief in Jesus. No insurmountable objections have been raised against faith by the famous thinkers of the modern era. Neither Karl Marx, nor Sigmund Freud, nor Charles Darwin, nor any of religion's critics from the worlds of literature and philosophy, has been left unanswered by equally competent and believing thinkers from the Christian community. Christians do not need to fear that the Gospels, composed so long ago, have become less applicable to people's lives as the generations pass. In fact, there is such a treasury of biblical commentaries available today that none of us can be excused from reading the Gospels on the ground that the Gospels are difficult to understand or foreign to our experience

One of the most frequently discussed Christological issues is the relation between Jesus' humanity and divinity. Throughout the history of Christian theology, the credal statement of the Council of Chalcedon (451) has generally been the customary theological point of departure for interpreting the mystery of Jesus.[17] But perhaps too much energy has been spent on the starting point. We have still never really clarified how Jesus could be "truly God and truly man." For the modern believer, the Creed of Chalcedon is not very illuminating when it says:

> We confess that one and the same Lord Jesus Christ, the only begotten Son, must be acknowledged in two natures, without confusion or change, without division or separation. The distinction between the natures was never abolished by their union but rather the character proper to each of the two natures was preserved as they came together in one person and one hypostasis.[18]

We should be grateful that contemporary theologians have tried to interpret this doctrine and explain what the Council meant by referring to "nature," "person," and "hypostasis." They have studied this teaching carefully because, for many Christians, belief in Jesus' divinity had obscured the reality of his being human. In other words, a widespread spiritual problem had arisen, for we were not paying sufficient attention to Jesus' being a truly human person. What happens to the richness of the Christian experience of God when believers are so caught by the divine Christ that they overlook the fact that it is in the ordinary, human situation of daily living that men and women become divinized? To underestimate the fullness of Jesus' humanity is to devalue God's presence in and through the humanity each of us carries, the routine circumstances in which we live, the events and struggles of our time. It is to blunt the impact of Jesus' walking through dusty villages, his dropping into people's homes and kitchens, his being thirsty, his calling ordinary, hardworking people to be disciples. It is to overlook the significance of the images and episodes from daily life which provide the material for Jesus' preaching and parables. Above all, it is to ignore God's full historical involvement with the human race and the power of the Gospel to challenge and transform our politics, our economics, and our social structures.

Sometimes people would read a Gospel passage where Jesus is reported not to know everything: "No one knows about that day or hour, not even the angels in heaven, nor the Son, but only the Father" (Mark 13:32). Or a text where Jesus was unable to work miracles: "He could not do any miracles there, except lay his hands on a few sick people and heal them" (Mark 6:5). And in both cases they would block the meaning of the texts by telling themselves that the Gospel writer was probably concealing the real facts. Those in-the-know would understand that Jesus, being divine, could do anything and that he certainly knew all things. After all, doesn't the Gospel of John tell us as much? The Fourth Gospel was often resorted to as the interpretative key for understanding the person of Jesus. And once you have confessed, with Thomas, that Jesus is your Lord and your God (John 20:28), what is the point of quibbling over clumsy details of the other Gospels which might downsize his divinity and remind us of his humanity?

Since I have raised the question about John's Gospel, I should like to answer it, though very briefly. John's Gospel presents a sustained theological and spiritual meditation on Jesus. But the Jesus portrayed there is not so much the historical, earthly Jesus whom we find, say, in the Gospel of Mark. The Jesus of John is the Jesus who is now present among his disciples, dwelling in their midst through the gift of the Spirit. The Jesus of the Fourth Gospel is the risen and glorious Lord; his life and preaching are pictured within the matrix of a highly developed faith. In other words, reading the Fourth Gospel is like watching a community's prayer unfold. That community was not concerned with historical questions about the pre-Easter Jesus; the Jesus to whom it related is now glorified and still doing his Father's work in the world. What is important, therefore, is not the information that Jesus is divine. What is important is that Jesus continues to do his Father's work among his brothers and sisters. We cannot grasp what Jesus' being divine means, in other words, apart from what Jesus did and continues to do for his disciples.

Now this idea, though extremely simple and dogmatically correct, keeps slipping from view. Apart from following Jesus, there is no way to appreciate what the Gospel of John is talking about. But there are people who claim to know that Jesus is God's Son and yet who do not live in a clearly recognizable way as disciples of Jesus. What then does their confession that Jesus is divine really mean? What do they have in mind in identifying themselves as Christian?

I leave my readers to answer these questions for themselves. Let me resume the thread of our discussion about how divinity ought not to be understood.

The Church's catechetical efforts to present its doctrine about Jesus are undermined by the popular assumption that everyone knows what being divine means. In fact, some people create the impression that they have a better grasp of what it means to be divine than they do of what it means to be human. The mistake is that, for many of us, being divine means being in control. We project an idea of divinity as power onto Jesus. Perhaps this projection stems from a distorted human desire to do marvels, to control our destiny, to have absolute power over life. Obviously, we do not possess such power, but we would relish sharing it. Since Jesus did marvelous deeds, however, he must have possessed such power. He even summoned the dead back to life, and he arose from death himself.

To be enticed by power, and to conceive of divinity as power, is the subtlest religious seduction. Adam and Eve yielded to it. Pursuing their notion of what being God was like, the human race "fell" from its innocence. "For God knows," advised the serpent, "that when you eat of it your eyes will be opened, and you will be like God, knowing good and evil" (Genesis 3:5). They ate the fruit, their eyes were opened, and they knew for the first time that they were naked. But the nakedness of Adam and Eve had been their natural state; it symbolized their always being open to the gaze of God. Nakedness represented their freedom from fear, for they were God's children. They had no need to cover themselves, since no thought, no action, no desire of theirs needed to be hidden from the eyes of God. Conversely, the nakedness of Jesus on the cross symbolized the absolute openness of this child of God to his Father's view. The crucified Jesus also represented the human being in its natural state, the state of freedom which comes from obedience.

Adam and Eve were tempted to grasp at divinity, and they fell from grace. Jesus commanded his disciples to be perfect, to be like God, for this was the way to their salvation. But the difference between the temptation and the command is two different understandings of what being like God means. For the first parents, it meant having knowledge, power, and control. For Jesus, divinity meant compassion, forgiveness, and love. And there is enough of the old Adam and Eve in us to crave power: but if we cannot have power, then it is enough for us that Jesus should have it. Thus we fashion Jesus into our god. Jesus will be the one who protects us against the insecurities, the anxieties, and the fear of death which threaten human existence. Jesus holds the power which we secretly envy; we stabilize ourselves against the insecurities of life by demanding that Jesus belong to us.

Yet even Jesus had to face Adam's temptation. To turn stones into bread, to win political control over Israel and the world, were the temptations by which the Gospel writers previewed the mission of Jesus. But Jesus was not going to be that kind of messiah; he would not pursue power, nor would he succumb to manipulating people into discipleship by a flashy display of miracles. Satan was denied the satisfaction of turning Jesus into a god. This drama was not lost on the early Church, either. The ancient hymn which appears in Paul's Letter to the Philippians celebrates the difference between the two Adams, God's first child and Jesus, both created after God's own image and likeness:

> Who, though he was in the form of God, did not count equality with God a thing to be grasped [as the first Adam had], but emptied himself, taking the form of a servant, being born in the likeness of men. And being found in human form he humbled himself and became obedient unto death, even death on a cross (Philippians 2:6–8 [Revised Standard Version]).[19]

On the one hand, we realize that Jesus was not simply a god, not even the living God. Christian faith believes Jesus to be God's Son, which is a very precise formulation of the relation between Jesus and the one he calls "Abba." On the other hand, we have to follow Jesus without benefit of miracles, dramatic calls from angels, transfigurations, or mighty signs like the multiplication of loaves or the raising of Lazarus. We have to discover Jesus' divinity in and through the ordinariness of human experience, both his and ours. I am suggesting that our reflection on Jesus needs to be guarded against a false notion of divinity. It may be that Jesus is not divine according to the way many people understand divinity. Divinity is not the projection of unfettered power, the ability to make the world run according to our norms of efficiency and success; death is not incompatible with the Christian notion of God. Human beings should not be frustrated because they are not divine. When we give voice to such frustration and disappointment, lamenting the fact that we have so little control over our own life and death, it may be the old Adam or the old Eve which is speaking. None of us would say that we want to be like God, the way Adam did. But our disorientation betrays us whenever we fashion our image of Jesus into the kind of being Adam and Eve were seduced into choosing.

4. Teacher, Example, and Savior

The disciple's relationship to Jesus unfolds in stages. For many of us, Jesus is the one whose instruction guides our living. When asked to state what the Lordship of Jesus signifies, we automatically define Jesus in terms of his being our teacher. And no wonder. All of us have gone to school and have had the experience of being taught, and out of that experience, naturally, we formed an image of Jesus. Similarly, all of us have observed certain individuals and been attracted to their style of speaking, acting, and relating to others. That too is part of human experience. Out of such experience, naturally, we create an understanding of Jesus as the model whose example we strive to imitate. What does it mean, therefore, to declare that Jesus is the Lord? It means that Jesus is both teacher and example.

But the Christian's faith in Jesus has to reach further. After all, we have had many teachers, and many people exemplify for us wholesome, authentic human living. What makes Jesus different from them? "Jesus," we answer, "is divine; Jesus is God's Son." But how do we come to this knowledge about Jesus? Out of what experience do we come to this conclusion? Indeed, the Christian tradition has bequeathed to us this doctrine of faith. But unless we have some experience upon which to build our image of Jesus as the Lord, does our acceptance of Jesus' divinity rest on a secure basis?

I raise this question because I discovered that a large number of students were unable to explain in a meaningful and coherent way why they claimed Jesus as their Lord and Savior. They would readily answer that Jesus died for their sins; but when asked further what "dying for sin" meant, they drew a blank. That Jesus died for human sin was, for many of them, a formula without meaning because it lacked a foundation in their personal experience. Since they were not present at the trial and death of Jesus, how could they intelligibly say that Jesus died for them? In the same way, while reading John 13 many people feel drawn to join Jesus as he sets about washing his disciples' feet. But, like Peter, they would be terribly embarrassed when Jesus stooped to wash their feet, if they have not yet grasped that Jesus must do something for us which we cannot do for ourselves. The footwashing is thus interpreted simply as an action to be imitated, for Jesus' example so obviously illustrates loving service. But the scene of Jesus washing his disciples' feet anticipates the later scene of his washing the disciples with his blood.

And the saving significance of the crucifixion scene is not so easily comprehended.

All of us know that we have sinned, but the problem is to relate that sinning to Jesus' cross. After all, one might argue, in some way or other all can be held responsible for the unjust deaths of virtuous people. Because of our negligence, our insensitivity, our failure to be politically and socially informed and involved, we must share the blame for the injustices which exist both in our society and in our world. Whenever the innocent are put to death, the ugliness of human cowardice and greed is exposed with its raw cynicism and hate. And in this way, their dying summons us to a sober examination of our values and behavior.

But to stretch this lesson across twenty centuries in order to locate its definitive illustration in the death of Jesus only starts to make sense if we already believe Jesus to be uniquely God's suffering servant. In other words, to say that Jesus is Lord and Savior because he died for our sins presupposes that we have already encountered him as the Lord. That is, Jesus' crucifixion, like the death of any innocent person, exposes the ugliness of sin, but his dying saves us because in it God has revealed that not even the ugliness of hatred, injustice, betrayal, or indifference will cancel God's love for the world. Since Jesus, who is the Lord, has died for our sins, the fear of being rejected forever by God, which fuels the tyranny of sin in human hearts, should have no hold on us. The Church knows that in Jesus God has saved us. Jesus is, therefore, the Savior of the world.

The basis of the Church's *knowledge* that Jesus is Lord is the resurrection. Unless Jesus had been raised, there would have been little inclination on the part of the disciples to see any special significance in the death of Jesus.

The *experience* out of which the Church proclaimed Jesus as Lord and Savior is its encounter with the risen Jesus who even today brings men and women to experience God's unconditional love and acceptance. The cross of Jesus remains the permanent sign in human history that God's relationship with the world is unbreakable, and the risen Jesus continues to be, for those who believe in him, the one in whom sinners experience the love of God, which surpasses all understanding. All of us have experienced being taught, and all of us have experienced being shaped by the example of others. But not all of us have experienced someone's loving us unselfishly and without any strings. Such love, by definition, is always of God. That accounts for why many do not realize what the divinity of Christ means. John writes: "God is love. Whoever lives in love lives in God, and God in him" (1 John 4:16). The Son is who he is because he has been loved by the Father, and through the Son that love is revealed and shared with the human race. Jesus lived in the Father, and the Father in him. Jesus proved this by letting the Spirit make him the forgiveness of God.

5. Jesus as the One Who Leads and Who Makes Human Communion Possible

There are a number of human relationships which serve as the basis of each believer's mode of imagining Jesus. Jesus can be brother, husband, or friend; for some, Jesus might embody the qualities of a mother or a sister or a wife. Behind the image there stands each one's faith experience: I experience Jesus as the one who accepts and embraces me, who teaches me, who listens to me, who heals painful memories, who shepherds me, who rescues me from selfishness, who transforms my hope.

Yet there are several other things Jesus does for us which are important and which help explain how God is acting in and through him. First, Jesus can be experienced as the one who leads, the one who is always ahead of us. The strength of this image comes from the fact that human life is, for many people, a journey. Without someone leading us, without reference points to locate whether we have made progress or whether we are merely wandering in a wilderness, the experience of journeying would give way to boredom, aimlessness, cynicism, and despair. Each person's life is a non-repeatable event, a one-time passage through this world. And somehow the wrong turns, the mistakes, the periods of idleness when we had lost any sense of direction, the encounters and accomplishments along the way, as well as the steady walking toward some real though obscure goal—everything seems to have its place when we begin to narrate our life stories. "These are the things," we would tell each other, "which happened to us along the way."

Second, Jesus can be experienced as the one who makes genuine human community possible. When two people who never knew each other meet, become friends, fall in love, and join their lives, communion has begun. But simply living together may do nothing to deepen their union. Unless they learn acceptance, patience, and how to share thoughts and feelings, unless they learn to forgive, to appreciate the depth and mystery in one another's soul, then they will not grow in that unifying love which is called communion. Now, if this is true when just two people are becoming friends, what is the likelihood that many men and women will come to know and accept each other as friends and companions? Those who followed Jesus soon discovered that their lives were joined, that their life stories formed part of a larger narrative. They experienced a closeness and communion among themselves, an inkling of what Jesus meant by the kingdom of God. In Jesus, they came to know others as fellow travelers, as companions who shared the same Spirit, as brothers and sisters whose common life was the breath of God. In Jesus, they learned the way of reconciliation and peace. Jesus enabled a new kind of human community by shaping the relationship among his disciples so that they knew themselves as sisters and brothers. To say, then, that Jesus leads and that Jesus creates human communion is to define further what his being divine means. Permit me to dwell on these two points for a few moments.

One evening I was talking with a young man who was thinking seriously about becoming a priest. During the course of the conversation, I asked him if he had ever considered being a missionary or joining a religious community. He replied that he was very close to his family and that he was thus more inclined to be a parish priest who would serve people in a small New England town near home. "Unless you're willing to walk with Christ to the ends of the universe," I found myself answering, "then you won't make your way even through your home town." With that response, I paused to reflect on what I had just said. Our conversation revealed to me that my own image of Jesus was "the one who leads." Jesus symbolizes all that is worth pursuing: his ideals, his way of seeing the world, his relationship with God, had in fact become my pearl of great price, the treasure buried in a field.

Human beings are so put together that they live out of and toward some picture of the world which, like a vision or a beam of light in the dark, lies ahead of them and illumines their path. Jesus represents everything worth living for, and this is something that cannot be said of any other human being. No one else, no human community, adequately embodies what another person might give his or her life for. For a vision is always larger than the individual who follows it and to some degree embodies it, and this also holds true in the case of Jesus. The light which irradiates the face of Jesus and silhouettes our image of him is the personhood of God. That is why, in following Jesus, the disciple is actually walking by God's own light. That is also why one's image of Jesus keeps changing. Or rather, that is why the circumstances of ordinary life—the people around us, our chores and responsibilities, the events in our neighborhoods and of our times, the thousands of things we observe, hear, and touch each day—keep assuming fresh color or meaning. The light of Christ highlights contrasts, it reveals shapes and forms, it dispels shadows: it discloses how a human life becomes beautiful by following the truth and goodness which is Jesus. The light of Christ renders the everydayness of things startlingly different, in much the same way that Jesus' parables turned everyday scenes inside out so that they revealed the secrets of the kingdom of God. To follow Jesus, then, is to risk losing everything for the sake of finding what one truly wants. Unless we are willing to stake everything, then we shall not discover our heart's desire even if it should appear in the most ordinary places and in the most routine activities. Jesus is the one who leads us toward God, and it is God's light that shines through the life and teaching of Jesus. He might not lead us any farther than our backyards and home towns; the physical distance of one's life journey does not matter. But there are men and women whose following of Jesus along an interior route has taken them across galaxies of inner time and space.

Jesus goes ahead of us. He has pioneered the way of faith and made the human pattern perfect. Jesus had eyes, he could hear, he walked and ate; he ran his hands through water, held children, made close friends, faced temptation. Jesus had faith, he prayed; he watched people languish in sickness and faced the inevitability of his own dying. Jesus had a native language and spoke with images and metaphors drawn from everyday experience; he chanted songs, he learned to read and to enjoy moments of quiet. Given the many images he used about banquets and wedding feasts, and the numerous occasions in which the Gospels depict him at table, Jesus appears to have delighted in parties and table fellowship. Jesus wept, and he died. From all this I am not simply underscoring the fact that Jesus was a human being. That is taken for granted. Rather, the fact that Jesus experienced all this affects the way we regard our own humanness. To see, to hear, to walk, to love, to rejoice, to laugh, to learn—the range and depth of human experiencing radiates the nearness of God because Jesus walked the human way before us. Or rather, Jesus goes ahead of us in seeing, in listening, in learning, in loving, in being with others, and in dying. To believe that Jesus is the one who leads is to admit that somehow one has begun to see as Jesus did, to speak and to touch as Jesus did, to think and dream as Jesus did. Or to put it even more directly, one has begun to put on the mind and heart of Christ. One can face the hardness of the world because Jesus is already there ahead of us. And one can face death, not because, after Jesus, one need not be afraid: the fear and the struggle remain. But Jesus went that way ahead of us, and because Jesus died, one can (as the apostle Thomas said) go and die with him.

In addition to imaging Jesus as the one who leads, we know him as the one who gathers us into the community of his disciples. Because of Jesus we are related to one another as men and women who know him, who belong to him, who love and follow him. And this makes us, as Jesus wanted it, sisters and brothers. Being-with-Jesus creates the possibility of looking at others and seeing them, not as strangers, nor as acquaintances and friends, but as family. For those who truly know Jesus, it is clear that we are more deeply related to one another in him than we are to those with whom we share the same parents. Every human relationship—mother to son, father to daughter, sister to brother, husband to wife, one friend to another—gives way to something which joins people from the bottom of their souls. From birth, all are children of God, although all do not see and grasp that reality. But one cannot be in the company of Jesus without becoming aware of his vision of the world, and I can think of nothing which is so unifying, so assuring, so richly human, as discovering others to be one's companions in the Lord.

I do not mean that because we are Christians, we automatically belong to a worldwide community called the Church. I do not mean we can pretend that every parish church houses a truly Christian community simply because the people there call themselves Christian. I do not mean that we can possibly relate to every Christian with the same degree of warmth and openness, any more than we can automatically assume that just because people live under the same roof and share the same meals, they are really experiencing a common life. Many people are too private; they neither can nor wish to share their inner lives with others. Many have never become aware of how much they need others, and their independence, or their lack of depth and self-knowledge, keeps them from being fully human and fully free. Many people experience God, but their religious experience, for one reason or another, remains unfinished. Still, all these people are our sisters and brothers.

What I mean is that we *can* come close to one another because of Jesus. Friendships can be formed, deepened, and maintained for life precisely because each of us knows, loves, and follows Jesus. This faith can be talked about, and in talking about it together, our faith grows clear and strong. We can pray together, and by praying we acknowledge how much we rely on one another for support, for forgiveness, and for discerning where Jesus is leading us. This prayer leads to a common life. Even though we do not share the same home, we are mindful of one another's needs, grateful for one another's talents, and committed to sharing our resources with the whole human family. From time to time, we come under the Lord's roof, listen together to his word, share in his table, and drink from the cup of his life. All of this, I say, is possible. And where it actually happens, there we know what the divinity of Jesus means. Jesus is the one who makes genuine human community happen. Gathered in his name, joined through his Spirit, the disciples of Jesus open their lives to one another. This would not occur if the light of Christ had not chased away fear—the fear of isolation, the fear of having one's shallowness uncovered, the fear of rejection, the fear of one's own capacity for holiness. This would not occur if the light of Christ had not brightened human desire—the desire to be loved for who we are, the desire for community, the desire for justice and peace, the desire to hear God call us by name.

If I had not experienced these things myself, then my grasp of Jesus as the one who enables community would be merely notional or theoretical. There are some teachings which I accept simply because I have been told that they form part of Christian faith. But the connection between Jesus and community must be experienced to be believed, for the divinity of Jesus is not a theoretical affair. Jesus' being divine is eminently practical and this-worldly: it means that Jesus is of God, and his being of God is—by his own words—linked with the fact that he makes his disciples one with himself and one with the Father. Without the experience, at some time in one's religious life, of knowing some men and women as friends in the Lord, would we not have failed to grasp the spiritual axis of human history? Would we not have missed the fact that God characteristically brings people together, urging them toward reconciliation and peace? And would we not have overlooked the significance of ordinary activities like being at table together, of making music together, of singing and dancing together, of working and struggling together, of laughing and praying together, of going to school together, of raising children together, of sharing dreams and, yes, even of sharing one another's dying? It is Jesus who pushes all these things into a wholly new light.

6. A Clarification about the Sinlessness of Jesus

The common picture of Jesus is very likely to be that of a perfect human being. Jesus is like us, we say, in all things except sin. As the Letter to the Hebrews puts it: "For we do not have a high priest who is unable to sympathize with our weaknesses, but we have one who has been tempted in every way, just as we are—yet was without sin" (4:15). Perhaps our imagination feels compelled to depict Jesus as sinless. Some Christians supposed that Jesus had to be sinless in order that his self-sacrifice to God should be a pure, acceptable offering for sin, although most of us today are not likely to think in such terms. Today, perhaps, many might say that we need an ideal to strive for and imitate, and so we fashion our picture of Jesus accordingly. The problem is that many Christians are then afflicted with a lifelong depression because each time they look at Jesus, they are reminded of how far they are from perfectly imitating his example. They meditate on the life of Jesus and always feel guilty by comparison. His sinlessness becomes an occasion for their feeling unworthy about who they are. And what is worse, they conclude that, although Jesus was like us, we shall never be like him.

To meet this difficulty we ought to recall several things. First, God created Jesus, not to make us feel guilty about being human, but to draw human beings in and through their humanity straight into the mystery of God. Jesus was a man so open to God's Spirit that the Spirit fully resided in him. Through this we learned that the divine aim for human nature is for all people to share the same Spirit. If one human being is capable of such grace, then, at least in principle, all human beings are. Second, I do not see how it could be *proven* that, except for Jesus, no human being was, is, or will be sinless. We simply do not have that sort of historical information about each and every human life. Surely, there have been other good and holy people. Surely, there are many others with whose lives God was well pleased. Yet I believe the Christian tradition's claim that Jesus was sinless, for I trust that the first disciples around Jesus found him to be without sin. They might not have expressed it that way, but they knew that they were sinners and they realized that in this matter Jesus was different from them.

Let me put it another way. Sin may be normal for human beings, but sin is not our natural state.[20] The fully human person does not sin, for the fully human person is not estranged from God. Jesus' union with the Father, therefore, is not what excepts him from the human condition. Rather, Jesus' openness to the Spirit, his union with God, is precisely what makes him fully human. And this is exactly what we are not, and we know it. We have yet to take full possession of our spontaneity and our freedom, and what is more, if we are honest with ourselves, we have to admit that we shall never become fully men and women without God's help. Jesus, the one who is "truly human," becomes a sign or promise that God's help will not be lacking to those who follow Jesus. How could we trust our own desire for holiness unless we knew that being holy, that is, being fully human, is a realizable possibility? In Jesus, God promises that each of us can be created into the divine image and likeness.

Sinlessness is not just a matter of never having sinned. Jesus could have died for us, after all, even if he had sinned sometime during his life. Other human beings have laid down their lives for their friends. Besides, some mentally handicapped people are probably subjectively incapable of doing anything morally wrong; they might be called innocent but usually no one calls them sinless. Nor are infants or young children capable of personal sin. For just as personal sin presupposes some measure of freedom, so also being sinless, it seems to me, requires personal freedom. In other words, sinlessness is nothing less than freedom made perfect, and herein lies something of a paradox. If the one who is free does not sin, then sinners are those who are not free. And if they are not free, how can they be held accountable for what they do?

The answer is that freedom is never given to us as a fully realized possibility. Indeed, we are not fully free, but that is because we are not yet fully created either. The hand of God still forms us. Are we then guilty of sin? Yes, though perhaps not always to the degree that we think, for many people suppose they are more free than they actually are. Inwardly, however, they are still victims of fear, of loneliness, and self-doubt. Karl Rahner observed: "We never know with ultimate certainty whether we really are sinners. But although it can be suppressed, we do know with ultimate certainty that we really *can* be sinners. . . ."[21] That is why I said *not always,* for people do run away from the hand that would form them. Sometimes they prefer to remain unfree, and therein lies the sin. To sin is to refuse the call to be our true selves; to sin is to choose to remain in a state which is not natural to human beings. And while sin and holiness, fear and freedom, admit of degrees, it becomes clear that the sinlessness of Jesus means he is an undistorted image of God. Jesus' being like us in all things except sin implies far more than that he never did anything wrong. It implies that the face of Jesus reflected the glory of God. And when we have fully clothed ourselves with the mystery of Christ, we too shall be without sin. Otherwise, what creative purpose does the Church's ministry of forgiveness serve?

Rather than speak of sinlessness, we might be better advised to talk about purity of heart or clarity of vision. When the inner eye is not distracted, when the heart's desire centers resolutely and undividedly on God, there you have a sinless person. To look at God with an unbroken regard for God's purpose and glory, God's desire and compassion, is to enjoy that wholeness of vision which characterized the life and teaching of Jesus. Referring to the sinlessness of Jesus is not all that helpful because a person could easily become preoccupied with his or her own sinfulness. Such preoccupation is spiritually distracting. Our first aim should be to see the world with a redeemed eye, as it were; to see the world and ourselves with purity of heart, as God sees.[22]

There is a basic religious supposition which states that there are only two spiritual postures. We can look at ourselves, or we can look at God. While the difference is elementary, it is frequently difficult to tell which posture one has adopted or from which perspective one is relating to the world. I have heard people say as they leave church on Sunday, "If the bishops support nuclear disarmament, I will stop contributing to the Church." And others: "Unless the Church ordains women, I am going to quit being Catholic." In cases like these, one has to ask: "What are you looking at—at yourself or at the Lord?" The examples can become far more complicated, particularly when they involve the nitty-gritty situations of daily life. But at bottom the fundamental issue remains one of clarity of vision or purity of heart: What are we attending to? An individual who crusades against poverty because he feels guilty about his own affluence is probably not attending to the Lord. The individual who continues to reach out to God even when she finds little evidence of God's concern is probably not looking at herself.

People often read the Gospels in order to discover what the moral demands of Jesus are, to learn what they ought to do. And while the Gospels do report what sort of behavior is expected of Jesus' disciples, to read them simply for their moral teaching indicates, it seems to me, an attitude of self-regard. It is hard to escape the trap of becoming preoccupied with being morally perfect or sinless. We can be trapped by our imperfection, our lapses of faith, our failures to love and to forgive. But it is altogether different to look at Jesus and to allow his light to displace the shadows of our fears, our pretexts and impatience, our shortness of vision and rashness of judgment. The religious trap, as St. Paul perceived so accurately, is to confuse sinlessness with a righteousness based on good works and obedience to ecclesiastical (and civil) laws. Sinlessness cannot be measured in terms of one's success at keeping moral precepts. For a person could fulfill every moral and religious obligation perfectly yet still not be looking at God.

This point was brought home to me through a remark made one Sunday morning after a sermon. Someone greeted me, "That was a wonderful sermon, Father; I feel terrible!" Making people feel guilty about themselves is one of the simplest things to accomplish in preaching, largely because most of us have so many things we regret about ourselves. Little skill is required for pointing out the proneness to sin, the personal inadequacy, the selfishness and anger which claim a hefty portion of our living. Often a sermon moves us only because it has tapped our feelings of guilt, and guilt arises because we realize that we have failed and that we have been caught, either by our conscience, by another person, or by the Lord.

Guilt, however, is not sorrow. Indeed, there are people who we wish would feel guilty about their behavior, but producing guilt was not part of Jesus' ministry of forgiveness, nor should it be part of the Church's. Guilt stems from having been found out, from having our sin uncovered and named. Sorrow, on the other hand, arises from having caught sight of Jesus. We are reminded of how much we mean to him; we remember his cross as the great sign of God's love for each of us. Genuine sorrow is a grace. The preacher cannot make people experience sorrow; he or she only prepares the way for God to act on the human heart. Since it is easier to induce guilt, many preachers settle for the simpler (and ungraced) result, probably without realizing what they have done.

The pressing spiritual challenge of the Church in any age, therefore, is to turn people's minds and hearts toward

God. Too often the Church has let itself become distracted by small ecclesiastical concerns, by speculative theological debates, by attempts to settle current moral problems, by political controversies, or even by sin itself. As a consequence, people have not been taught to notice what God is like. Since it is less troublesome to say what God is not, and since those who know God intimately are not always the ones who teach and preach, the Church succumbs to the temptation to speak and preach about things other than God.

Yet God is what religion is all about: the God whom we believe creates the world in and out of every moment, the God whose love brought the universe into being and which constantly renews human lives, the God whose thinking and loving have been revealed in the person of Jesus. To this God human eyes must be directed. No problem, no matter how serious it appears, should be approached apart from looking at God. Isolated from the light of Christ, evil assumes menacing proportions; morality becomes cold and brittle. The overriding question for those who seek purity of heart is: Where is the Lord?

For the person who is looking at Jesus, the issue is not, for example, whether Jesus forbids his disciples to own property, but what kind of God Jesus was revealing such that distinctions of social class and income are recognized as obstacles to knowing the Lord. Or again, the issue is not how many times the brother or sister can reasonably expect our forgiveness, but what sort of God Jesus experienced such that the question about the kinds and frequency of sin loses its significance altogether.

People do not become holy merely by examining their consciences, discovering their sins and imperfections, and resolving to improve their actions. Men and women become perfect and holy by contact with the living God. No one reaches holiness without looking regularly and steadily on Jesus. When sin does not succeed in keeping us from God by chaining us to some evil action or desire, it conquers by another strategy. Sin distracts the disciple by showing itself as the obstacle which must be overcome before one can be perfect. If sin cannot enjoy complete claim over our minds and wills, then at least it can rob us of the prize of seeing God with a pure heart by entangling us in the pursuit of perfection. We get lost in a maze of failures, evil inclinations, and feelings of guilt or personal inadequacy. Like Peter trying to walk on the waves, once we start attending to the chaos around us by taking our eyes off Jesus, we sink into our own shortness of vision and faith.

I have discussed the matter of sinfulness and guilt at some length because our ordinary notion of sinlessness obscures the divinity of Jesus. Just as many people confound divinity with power, so too they confuse sinlessness with the ability to avoid sinning. Just as they know themselves not to be all powerful, they know that they are incapable of putting an end to sin in themselves. But sinlessness, I have argued, is purity of vision; it comes from having one's eyes on God. "Blessed are the pure in heart," Jesus said, "for they will see God." In Jesus' case, this is not a grace promised but something fulfilled. Jesus sees God because he is free, and he is free because the Spirit had rushed into him: God created Jesus this way. But the sinlessness of Jesus is not intended to make us feel guilty by comparison, for that would give the final victory to the power of sin. The sinlessness of Jesus pledges God to make us free, to purify our vision: and this happens insofar as we look at Jesus and contemplate that face which is brightened by the glory of God.

7. The Changing Face of Jesus

I have already mentioned the fact that at different periods in the history of Christian faith, as well as at various points in their lives, Christians have been attracted to one or another Gospel text or some particular image of Jesus. Although Jesus died comparatively young, old people relate to him, perhaps pondering a text like that of Jesus to Peter: "I tell you the truth, when you were younger you dressed yourself and went where you wanted; but when you are old you will stretch out your hands, and someone else will dress you and lead you where you do not want to go" (John 21:18). Women have to relate to Jesus affectively, and so do men, with all the psychological challenges which this invites. Children too will have their images of Jesus; Jesus is the one who welcomes them and holds them before his disciples as examples of innocent trust. Certain images appeal to us when we have sinned or lost our way; other texts strike us when we are feeling the urge to withdraw for quiet, solitary prayer. Other images and texts of the Gospels attract us when we are moved to do something courageous for God's sake, or when we sense ourselves to be especially loved, called, and chosen by Jesus.

All this is understandable. Each of us displays a variety of faces depending upon whom we are meeting, the time and circumstances of our conversations, the needs and backgrounds of our friends, and so on. We relate one way to a husband or wife, another way to a close friend, still another way to children, an employee, or a rich uncle. Each new situation, each person draws something else out of us: we do not literally become all things to all people, but we may come close.

So also with Jesus. For some he becomes father or brother; for others he becomes sister, mother, or husband. Jesus appears one way to the non-Christian and another to the enslaved or persecuted disciple. There are numerous possibilities. The face of Jesus changes for each of us as we mature in discipleship.

Yet if the face of Jesus changes, so do we. If the word of God is heard differently at particular times and places in our lives, then that word is also becoming flesh in us, purifying and molding us into the daughters and sons of God. Let us consider the doctrine of the incarnation in reverse, as the mystery which illumines who and what we are rather than who and what Jesus is. Primarily, incarnation means that the word of God becomes flesh, as the Gospel tells us (John 1:14). This means several things. The word becomes material at the dawn of creation when God speaks and the word of God orders all things into their place, separating light from darkness, order from chaos, one living thing from another. The word of God also becomes historical. It enters human history, fashioning nations and their destinies, instructing them on the difference between the way of life and the way of death. The word of God becomes flesh and blood in Jesus. Through Jesus God has uttered a life-giving, creative word about what human beings are, for what purpose they have been made, how they are to live and how they are to die. But finally, the word of God would be fruitless and unavailing unless it also took flesh in us who hear and believe it. "That Christ may dwell in your hearts through faith," says the Letter to the Ephesians (3:17). Again, Paul writes: "Do you not know that you are God's temple and that God's Spirit lives in you?" (1 Corinthians 3:16). And Jesus says in John's Gospel: "I am in my Father, and you are in me, and I am in you" (14:20). A little later: "If anyone loves me, he will obey my teaching. My Father will love him, and we will come to him and make our home with him" (John 14:23).

The word of God is becoming incarnate in us: this is the miracle of our creation. Looked at in reverse, therefore, the incarnation discloses the mystery which we are. The changing face of Jesus becomes the changing face of Christ in us. The word of God becomes material and historical; it takes on flesh and blood, it becomes spiritual in human beings. That word finds its home in us, drawing order and beauty out of the chaos of our tangled feelings, runaway desires and self-centeredness. The Spirit of God hovers over our lives, forming us into the image and likeness of God, which is Christ. As the Spirit works, the image of Christ in us matures, clarifies, deepens, and grows strong. "God has chosen to make known among the Gentiles," Paul wrote, "the glorious riches of this mystery, which is Christ in you, the hope of glory" (Colossians 1:27).

If people should approach us with the request to show them Jesus so that they might believe in him, we might answer, paraphrasing the Gospel text: Anyone who has seen us, has seen Jesus. How can you say, "Show me Jesus?" Don't you realize that we are in Jesus and that Jesus is in us? The words we speak are not just our own. Rather, it is Jesus, living in us, who is doing his work (see John 14:8–10). We would not presume to say that we are Jesus, any more than Jesus presumed to say that he was the Father. But Jesus was one with the Father, and the disciple is called to be one with Jesus. Each Christian life becomes a word of God uttered into the world. As that word takes flesh in our lives, our whole being proclaims more and more clearly one word: Jesus!

Finally, the word of God also becomes Church. To conclude our understanding of God's formative grace in the world at the point of our personal creation would be premature. God is also fashioning a people. The Spirit hovers over individuals, drawing them to desire unity, prompting them to work for others, assisting them to remember the words and example of Jesus. Incarnation and Pentecost are linked. The only way to comprehend why God entered our world comes from realizing that there is no other way to rescue the possibility of genuine human community, and creating community is the work of the Spirit. The Church also has its changing face, as its own proper mystery unfolds. Laying aside the desire for prestige, or power, or moral control over people's lives; learning how to seek out and save sinners, as Jesus did, with understanding and compassion; refusing to offer its own brand of certitude and authority when people are looking for living bread and living water: through this the Church changes. The word of God finds its home in the midst of the Church, pitching its tent there and abiding among the people of God.

What can the Christian say about Jesus? We can say that in Jesus God was one of us. In Jesus, the world was being reconciled to God. Jesus is the one who leads, powerlessly and sinlessly, trusting totally in God and fully free. Wherever we are along our life's journey—children, teenagers, young adults, middle-aged people, old men and women—Jesus is ever ahead of us. That is the way I image him, changing yet steady too, as I change and my faith deepens. Jesus is also the one who draws us into the company of his disciples. This community is not restricted to people from our own families, to our local church, not even to the universal Church. Such lines of demarcation—family, neighborhood, religious community, official

Church—do not prevent Jesus from drawing us into an ever more profound companionship of faith and love.

To Summarize

In the course of this chapter we have been reflecting on the reality which Jesus is for us. We began by noting that a number of factors—cultural, historical, personal—condition our image of Jesus, and it is important to be aware of them. While there is plenty of theological room for a diversity of images, we must guard against bending Jesus to suit our ideas and choices and not allowing him to challenge us. Being-with-Jesus calls for a change of loyalty; it means throwing in one's lot with the kingdom of God, which Jesus represents. Since one of the ideas we impose on Jesus is a notion of divinity conceived as power, it was necessary to explain what being divine does not mean. We purified the notion of divinity further by suggesting that the sinlessness of Jesus is not so much a trademark of his being divine but of his being fully, authentically human. What then does the divinity of Jesus mean? It seems to me that one way of answering this question is to reflect on what Jesus continues to do among us. Jesus transforms human hope, drawing us further into the whole human family. Jesus makes the faithfulness and compassion of God really present: he saves us by rescuing our capacity to forgive and to love. Finally, in whatever place we are along our life's journey, Jesus is always there ahead of us: Jesus is the one who leads and who makes genuine communion among men and women possible.

I have avoided any speculative and metaphysical consideration of Jesus' relationship to God. When theologians delve into the mystery of the union between God and Jesus, they often generate more heat than light. Anyone who tries to follow Jesus with all her heart, soul, mind, and strength, has already declared her faith in the divinity of Jesus. Anyone who allows Jesus to lead him into the circle of God's concerns and who struggles, precisely because he is with Jesus, to bear witness to God's love for the world, has already confessed that Jesus is Lord. Yet it is God who appears in and through the face of Jesus; through that face Christians are continually drawn to love the God they cannot see.

2

Do I Have a Soul Worth Saving?

> The strange mistrust I had of myself, of my own being, has flown, I believe for ever. That conflict is done. I cannot understand it any more. I am reconciled to myself, to the poor, poor shell of me. How easy it is to hate oneself! True grace is to forget. Yet if pride could die in us, the supreme grace would be to love oneself in all simplicity—as one would love any of those who themselves have suffered and loved in Christ (Georges Bernanos, *The Diary of a Country Priest*).

One of the great personal discoveries made by the young St. Augustine, as we learn from his *Confessions,* was that there was no way he could arrive at self-knowledge without inquiring about God. Or, to put the insight another way, knowledge of self and knowledge of God were correlative. As Augustine realized more clearly and precisely who he was, he understood that who and what human beings are makes little sense apart from the God who is already within them. For Augustine, God was the ultimate intellectual light which makes inner vision possible, and he was fond of quoting the verse, "In your light we see light" (Psalm 36:9). God was also the great love which wound its way through every one of Augustine's desires. Even in his sinning, Augustine came to see that he was running away from the God his soul secretly loved. Thus, in a wonderful irony of grace, the sinner was always affirming the existence of God. But Augustine did not actually know God directly. Rather, in coming to understand who he was, Augustine experienced himself as one who was always being known by God.

Along with many an ancient thinker, Augustine took for granted that there were two spheres of reality, the material and the spiritual. They disputed about which of the two was, from a practical point of view, the more important for us. But the human soul fell clearly into the category of spiritual things. Since the only thing capable of escaping the chains of physical existence and surviving death was a spiritual substance like the soul, saving one's soul naturally became one's major life-project. The dangerous side-effect of this dedication to saving one's soul was a tendency to ignore or to devalue material creation. Although the Word had become flesh in Jesus, the ancient Christian was not likely to interpret this doctrine as affirming the nobility and goodness of materiality. On the contrary, the Son of God descended into our condition in order to draw us with him into the spiritual realms of God's glory. Theology in the twentieth century is remarkable for its positive assessment of the material world and its readiness to interpret the incarnation as God's commitment to flesh and blood, and as a promise that a redeemed creation will occupy a permanent place in God's sight.

What bothers me about this distinction between spirit and matter is the apparent inconsistency of a spiritual being creating a material universe. What is the point of fashioning a material universe if the final destiny of men and women is their spiritual existence with God? Doesn't it appear that the labor of creating a material world is, in the long run, an enormously unnecessary expenditure of energy on God's part? Isn't the physical universe merely provisional? After all, angels enjoy a spiritual existence without having been routed first through materiality. Besides, if materiality is somehow essential to our becoming fully spiritual creatures, how does God manage to be a spiritual being? Wouldn't matter also be important for God?

Admittedly, these questions will strike many Christians as far-fetched. Not only are such concerns quite removed from the thinking and living of ordinary believers, but how in the world can one hope to answer them?

I would agree that questions like these ultimately cannot be solved. There is a great deal about the physical universe—its origin, many details of its development, its eventual state—that we do not know. How then could we expect to fathom the mystery of God? As Job learned, no one can make God stand before the bar of human reason. Yet the exercise of chewing over such questions can be fruitful, I believe, because it may lead to deeper self-knowledge. Following Augustine's insight, as we discover more about ourselves (and about our world), we also move closer to God. In fact, Augustine never wearied of pondering questions about creation, as anyone who has struggled through the last three books of the *Confessions* is aware. Was there always a creation, and if not, what was God doing before time began? And what is time? What is meant by "the beginning"? Augustine was a thinking Christian. His life demonstrates that the mind has its own spiritual journey to make, just as the heart does. The mind's journey starts with pondering the world as we find it.

The Work of Creation Continues

The human mind will not tolerate the idea that the universe simply burst into existence without any antecedent cause. Therefore, we conclude, something has to be eternal. Something always had to be "there," whether matter, energy, or God. Traditionally, Christian theology has held that God created the physical universe "from nothing." The idea of a universe spontaneously bursting into existence made no sense, and matter alone, being finite, could not account for its own existence. Without debating this position, let us consider another possibility.

What prevents us from supposing that matter in some form simply existed, that the universe gradually evolved into its present form, and that one day, when all its energy is spent, the universe will become dark, silent, and cold? This thought may sound intellectually frightening, but the idea is not downright impossible. After all, something always existed. Why couldn't that something be matter or energy? And what would keep that matter or energy from finally being exhausted? To anyone who objected that the prospect is unreasonable, we might respond, "Unreasonable to whom? That is how the universe is."

Next, try to comprehend the meaning of the statement "Something always existed." To keep this thought in our heads for more than a few moments is troublesome. It requires an effort that strains and wearies the mind. Trying to think how something simply was, is, and always will be leaves the mind reeling. How can a fact be its own explanation? And yet, some fact does explain itself; something does exist as a sheer matter of fact. But if the universe had no beginning, we reason to ourselves, then why should it have an end? And if it were to be endless, would such a universe make the notion of God unnecessary? Would the eternity of matter be any more unreasonable than the notion of an ever-existing God?

Now, while I believe that God is the ultimate horizon within which the universe needs to be understood, I would not want to present my belief in such a way that God merely substitutes for a plausible physical explanation for the existence of the universe. God should not be invoked in order to answer questions about the physical universe which science has so far been unable to figure out. The scientific answers, in fact, might never be reached, given the constraints upon what we can observe and measure about the universe. Yet this does not mean that scientific answers are in principle unobtainable. In other words, we cannot leap to metaphysics or to theology to fill in the gaps in our understanding of the physical world. If the universe as we know it began with a "big bang," as many scientists today believe, then that fact alone would not warrant our concluding that God created the universe some twenty billion years ago, according to human reckoning, by commanding a mighty "Let there be light." Arguing to God's existence is never that simple. The human mind would still want to know what was "there" to explode in the first place. Perhaps the universe persists over incredibly long periods of alternating states of expansion and contraction. At any rate, God cannot be reduced either to a metaphysical first principle or to a scientific hypothesis developed by religiously minded people. The fact that God is the Creator, I would urge, does not explain the existence of the universe. Or, to state the point a bit differently, theological understanding and scientific understanding represent two distinct ways of knowing the world. They may be complementary at times, but religion and science should not be confused. Not every scientist is a believer, a fact which ought to persuade us that the universe speaks of God only to those who have already discovered the holy mystery which dwells in their hearts and minds. Christian theology accepts the existence of the universe as a fact, and it interprets that fact—it does not account for it scientifically—in the light of the community's story about the God who has been revealed as the Father of Jesus Christ. To say that God creates is to make a statement of faith, and to refer to the universe as creation is to interpret the material world religiously.

The reader may be relieved to know that I do not intend to pursue these considerations very far. I have raised them in order to draw attention to an underlying problem in our thinking about God and creation. The mind tends to slip in and out of time. It tends to consider things at one moment from the framework of eternity and at another moment from the framework of space and time, at one moment from the point of view of theology or philosophy, and at another moment from the point of view of the natural sciences. This is a basic difficulty. It also means that we tend to slide back and forth between the notions of spirit and matter: God, eternity, and spirit fall on one side of our thoughts; materiality, history, mortality, and flesh fall on the other side. Reflecting on these things is made easier, however, if we start by clarifying, from a theological perspective, what is meant by "the beginning."

The phrase "in the beginning" connotes a particular moment in time, but since the days of the early Christian writers it has been recognized that the phrase does not refer to temporality. "Scripture is not speaking here of any temporal beginning," Origen wrote in his first homily on Genesis, "but it says that the heaven and the earth and all things which were made were made 'in the beginning,' that is, in the Savior."[1] Augustine, too, interpreted the phrase in terms of Christ: "For, when Scripture says, 'In the beginning God created heaven and earth,' by the name of 'God' we understand the Father, and by the name of 'Beginning,' the Son, who is the Beginning, not for the Father, but first and foremost for the spiritual beings He has created and then also for all creatures."[2]

The common sense meaning of the phrase is that creation took place at some moment billions of years ago when God spoke an almighty "Let there be" into the emptiness of space and suddenly matter appeared. The development of the universe since then can be measured in terms of ages and years; we can estimate how many billions of years passed before the earth became hospitable to life. Everything "before" the beginning belongs to eternity.

But trying to think in terms of a before and after the moment of creation is a misguided effort. The mind cannot move inside and outside of time, or from eternity into time, as if eternity were only a different kind of time. Before the beginning, in other words, there was nothing. There was only "the beginning," and the reason why the mind becomes frustrated in attempting to penetrate to something behind the beginning is that there was (and is) nothing there to grasp. It would make no sense to puzzle over why God created the cosmos at one particular instant rather than another.

From a theological point of view, therefore, "in the beginning" could be located at every moment. The beginning could have been twenty billion years ago; it could have been ten billion years ago; it could be now. If the beginning marks the start of God's creative work, then we should go on to say that God's creative work is always starting. From a human standpoint, one speaks of past, present, and future. One thinks of creation (at the beginning), providence (the present unfolding of God's creative design), and the consummation (the fulfillment of the divine initiative). Yet from a divine standpoint, if we can be bold enough to imagine it, there is only the present. God is always the Creator, always the guiding hand, always the goal and fulfillment. Even the theological scheme which attributed creation to the Father, redemption to the Son, and sanctification to the Spirit was limited in this regard. The life-sharing activity of God cannot be dated; God does not conform to our schemes of past, present, and future. God is always creating, always redeeming, and always making creatures holy.[3] Maybe that helps explain why Jesus told the Sadducees: "But about the resurrection of the dead—have you not read what God said to you, 'I am the God of Abraham, the God of Isaac, and the God of Jacob'? He is not the God of the dead but of the living" (Matthew 22:31–32).

What was going on before the beginning? Nothing. Did matter always exist? Perhaps, but we cannot prove it. Does God always exist? Yes, but the reasons which confirm a person's belief in God are to be found in the present, in the everyday world of human living, and not in the distant past. Those reasons are located in the way order is still being evoked out of the chaos which exists in the minds and hearts, the lives and experiences of men and women here and now. Is eternity different from time? Yes, but the difference is qualitative, not quantitative or numerical.

One implication of this attempt to recenter our thinking about creation in terms of a divine standpoint is that we would not be able to tell the difference between a creation which occurred instantaneously, or in seven days, or over billions of years. From God's point of view, everything happens now. Human beings measure according to hours, years, even light years, and we date events in terms of past and future. But not so with God. The whole material world, with all its struggle, achievement, and beauty, is for God like a thousand years: "For a thousand years in your sight are like a day that has just gone by, or like a watch in the night" (Psalm 90:4). I do not wish to downplay the value of human history, but I do think it is important to notice the limitations of our ordinary frames of reference. Many people regard traveling around the globe as quite an accomplishment. But what is so astounding about earth travel compared to a space flight to the moon, or a satellite speeding toward Jupiter and on through the vast distance between galaxies? A few steps toward one's next-door neighbor can be more significant than an interstellar voyage, unless, of course, one is impressed by sheer numbers of miles. The huge numbers of galaxies, stars, and planets which comprise the universe can mesmerize us, but why should we be overawed by the cosmic scale of things? A few moments in which one learns to swallow one's pride and ask for forgiveness count far more importantly than a billion years, unless, of course, one thinks of time as a huge series of blanks in which events are inserted, regardless of their kind or quality.

We could make similar observations with respect to space and matter. Ever since astronomers demonstrated that the earth does not lie at the center of the universe, human beings have been bothered by the possibility that our existence might be incidental to the universe as a whole. But the telescope reveals only that the earth is not positioned at the geometrical center of the cosmos. We should not imagine that God creates the world like a human architect, using ruler and compass; geometry is our invention. From a divine standpoint, in other words, any place can be the center. Or perhaps it would be more accurate to say that our notion of the spatial center is anthropomorphic. Once we realize this, then our picture of the universe can be stabilized in terms of where the human being meets God, for in that place the human center, the real center, the center which truly matters, ought to be located. Likewise, human builders are careful not to waste time and materials. Thus, from a human perspective it appears that outlandish amounts of time, energy, and matter were spent before the tiny planet which is our home emerged. But again, to imagine that God might have fashioned the world more economically is to impose an anthropomorphic measure on divine creative activity. We are not in a position to determine whether God has worked efficiently in creating our world. Once we become aware of this, then the size and mass of the universe will not shadow us into insignificance. What counts is the stuff which makes us human, which builds our history, which enables us to think, and to choose, and to love. If the mind can be dazzled by the expanse of the cosmos, it should be amazed even more by a world enriched with life, culture, holiness, and grace.

Now this does not solve the problem about why a spiritual being would fashion a material universe. In attempting to settle this difficulty, I would suggest that the categories of matter and spirit are not adequately descriptive from a divine standpoint. Yes, these categories make sense as ways of interpreting our experience, just as it makes sense for us to use calendars and clocks. Yes, matter and spirit are convenient terms for measuring the difference between lower and higher nature, just as it is convenient for us to measure the physical world in terms of meters, miles, and light years. Yes, the Bible speaks of God's breathing the divine spirit into our nostrils, and when that spirit is withdrawn, we die. But does it make sense to imagine God creating physical bodies and then placing within them a spiritual substance or soul? Human beings, after all, are not manufactured; they are created. And creation is never instantaneous, except perhaps from God's point of view. Spirit, in other words, needs to be created, just as matter does. It is a whole person which God fashions: God does not create a body and a soul (that is our way of describing and measuring). God creates a man or a woman; to make us fully human, that is, to ensoul us, generally requires a lifetime. And furthermore, we have no means of determining in our own case or in the case of any other man or woman whether God's creating us has proceeded efficiently, economically, and smoothly. Stories of grace cannot be judged by ruler and compass, or by calendars and clocks.

Christians do not believe that God created the human being, body and soul, and then placed it in the world to achieve salvation by its native power. Human beings are understood to stand in constant need of God's grace, which might be imaged as the divine breath, for God is always breathing divine life and spirit into us. Without God's continual care, we would falter and collapse, dropping into the earth from whence we came. We might not have spoken this way in the past, but we always believed that God's creative action was ongoing, for we strongly insisted upon the daily necessity of divine grace. Life on earth cannot be summed up as a great test which we have to pass before entering our eternal reward, even though some presentations of the salvation story boiled down to this. Rather, life should be viewed as the time and place where people have to find God, not only once but every day. The face of this God changes as men and women become more fully people of faith. Our preferred biblical text for prayer is generally not the story of Eden, with its command, its test, and its fall from grace. Instead, we are drawn to texts like Jeremiah 18, with the scene of the pot-

ter and his clay, or to Psalm 139, with its serene confidence in God's ever-present care, or to Luke 24:13–35,
the story of the disciples on the Emmaus road whose eyes
were opened by a Jesus who was walking with them but
whom they did not at first recognize. These are passages
about being formed, about being known, about being
taught by a really present, though sometimes unrecog-
nized Lord. They are passages which help us to interpret
human existence. They reflect a spirituality which is cre-
ation-centered.

A theological perspective which centers on creation
takes its point of departure from a biblical image like the
Spirit hovering over the face of the deep, or the potter
with his hands pressed into the clay. It presents a vision in
which the creative action of God is always foremost. Creation, redemption, and sanctification are all aspects of a
single divine outreach, the pressure of God's creative
hands. Teilhard de Chardin once wrote:

> In the life springing up within me, in the material ele-
> ments that sustain me, it is not just your gifts that I
> discern: it is you yourself that I encounter, you who
> cause me to share in your own being, and whose hands
> mould me. In the initial ordering and modulating of
> the life-force which is in me, and in the continuous,
> helpful action upon me of secondary causes, I am in
> very truth in contact—and the closest possible con-
> tact—with the two aspects of your creative activity; I
> encounter and I kiss your two wonderful hands: the
> hand that lays hold on us at so deep a level that it
> becomes merged, in us, with the sources of life, and
> the hand whose grasp is so immense that under its
> slightest pressure all the springs of the universe
> respond harmoniously together.[4]

No one except God observed the dawn of the cosmos, but each of us has an immediate experience of his or her own creation. We can review the moments and events of our lives in which we know our spirits to have been teased into action, or tempered, or made strong. The fuss and troubles of daily life, the struggle of making hard decisions, dealing with error and sin, not to mention our habit of looking back at the past and piecing together the main scam of our life story—all these things provide clues about what it means to be created. We experience the process of being fashioned or formed. When a person is able to regard the events and moments of life through the eyes of faith, then the various things which happen to him are revealed as the finger of God working over the clay, or the breath of God blowing life and form into what otherwise appears trivial, meaningless, and unconnected. No event, no moment, no detail, no daydream or desire, no thought or encounter, is unrelated to the process of our being made.

The creative process is not something passively endured, either. We play our part. We respond to the particular set of circumstances which make up our lives. We make our mistakes, we enjoy our small triumphs and some major victories. And what is happening through it all? Our freedom is becoming pure. Our desiring grows increasingly directed toward wanting to do what is good and to loving what is right. Our inner vision sharpens so that we learn to see God. Throughout our lives, the human soul is being formed. The breath of God fills the cavities of our spirit, the chambers of our minds and hearts.

And so, human beings will continue to study, explore, and ponder the physical universe, for we are intelligent and inquisitive creatures. The universe will keep enticing us into questioning and exploring ourselves, since human origins merge with the energies and origins of the cosmos. The Christian philosopher or theologian might be able to derive the existence of the universe from the fact of God's creative activity, but one does not come to acknowledge God's creative activity simply on the basis of the fact that the universe exists. The holy mystery of God already surrounds us, enclosing both the human mind and the human heart. Once we awaken to this presence, once we experience the creative action of God in our lives, then God can be glorified for creation and the universe tells of the divine greatness. Writers such as Origen and Augustine, who devoted considerable attention to thinking about creation, did not raise in the same way the points we have been making, but I don't think that they would disagree, at least not from the vantage point they enjoy now.

The Human Soul

What, then, is the human soul?

Imagine, for a moment, an event which is personally very meaningful, one that we would like to save. How might we go about preserving it? We might describe it in a diary, or tape-record it, or photograph it. The event itself, however, will always belong to the past. It can be recalled, of course. And if others shared the same experience, then in the retelling the event is in some way re-experienced. But the moment is re-experienced only as a shared memory. The sharing or retelling is a new moment; the original event belongs to the past. Events, in other words, cannot be saved like stamps, souvenirs, photographs, diaries, and so on, because events are not things or objects but occurrences or happenings.

To be really precise, even things can be looked upon as events. This is so, not merely because on a sub-atomic level, as physicists have discovered, everything is in motion, but also because every object has to take its place as part of the past. Walking through a museum confirms the point. The objects are "there" but they belong to another time and place; they no longer have living connections in the present. The abandoned doll or sled, clothes which have passed out of fashion, a broken lawn mower, scenes of an old neighborhood, a high school diploma, and so on—such things are like events. They can be stored away in garages and scrapbooks, yet once they join the past, they only remind us that material things are always perishing. The value or meaning we attach to things changes over time, for the objects themselves are merely signposts along the lanes of our memory. We need them to keep from forgetting who we are and where we have come from.

The human being is also an event, not a thing or an object. So also the human soul, that which is specifically human about us, is not a thing, an object, or even a spiritual substance. Our conviction that every human being has a soul is another way of stating that we hold all human life to be sacred, because it comes from God. Belief in the soul underwrites the basic equality which all human beings share. The soul is not to be confused with the self or the ego. Soul refers to that about human beings which is most worth saving from death and decay. It also designates that capacity for perfection and growth by which human beings become divine. The soul of a villain is different from the soul of a saint, and the soul of a fetus is not the same as the soul of a free, loving, responsible adult.

The human soul is that dimension about us which can be remembered by God. Not our looks, not our bodily shape and size, not our brain or our memory. While the soul cannot be equated with self-consciousness, the soul is not independent of our individual identities, either. The soul means what God can save; it is what makes us, as men and women, truly good and thus capable of being loved. Soul includes the genuine achievement of a lifetime, which God alone knows from inside of us. Others may have observed greatness in the way we acted or spoke, but they seldom see (and then only indirectly) what takes place in the human heart. Conversely, while we notice how many times another person stumbles and falls, only God sees the struggling that went on before the fall, and only God knows how many times that person tried to stand up again.

Since the soul refers to what God holds on to, real human achievement is not lost through illness which impairs consciousness, or through senility, or through any other form of diminishment. God remembers us at our best, and our best self is ever present to God. God constantly beholds us in our prime, as it were. It would make no sense for God to remember our sin; that would not serve any creative purpose. Rather, God sees the achievement of our hearts, our growing readiness to forgive and to serve selflessly, for this is what constitutes the beauty of the human form. Origen and Augustine were wonderfully correct, therefore, when they identified "the beginning" with Christ. We are always being made "in the beginning"; that is, we are always being fashioned into the image and likeness of God, which is Christ. Christ is the first principle of creation.

Our understanding of the soul, then, needs to incorporate not only what we are by our birth, but also what we become by our living. What is the most beautiful thing one can imagine? Finally, I think, it is the person who has been grasped by love. No piece of jewelry, no work of art or music, no landscape, brilliant idea, or technological feat, compares with the beauty of a heart which has become selfless, compassionate, and free. Being joined to God is the final stage in our creation as persons. The soul would perish—that event of living which each of us is—unless God personally drew us into the divine mystery and remembered our goodness. Our sin, on the other hand, is not something which can be rescued, for sin is not something that the hands of God can hold. To be remembered by God, then, means to be held forever within the divine life, in a union so complete that it surpasses all human relationships and love. Apart from God, human achievement would be lost and forgotten. Those who have led heroic lives but whom the world never noticed would count for nothing in the balance of history. And history itself would one day be swept away when the last human being dies.

It is faith and an intuition which prevent us from losing our way altogether. We believe that the life of Jesus, and the lives of those who follow him, indicate the true and proper meaning of existence. Every creative process in the universe comes to a climax in the capacity of rational beings for freedom, and freedom becomes perfect through love. And the intuition? The intuition is that the universe cannot be understood by looking backward to its origins, or within to its basic physical laws, or ahead to its projected final state. The universe has to be understood by looking around us and noticing the incomprehensible mystery unfolding in our midst. "In the beginning" is today. It is every day. The beginning is the point where God says, "Let there be light." "And," the biblical narrative continues, "it was so . . . and that life was the light of men . . . and the darkness has not overcome it." Creation is always beginning afresh, for God never stops uttering the creative word.

Matter and Spirit

When I was studying philosophy as part of seminary training, we had to learn a thesis to the effect that the human soul was naturally immortal. This conclusion could be reached, according to Scholastic philosophy, by the use of reasoning apart from revelation. It surprised me to learn, while studying theology, that the people of Israel (to whom God had been revealed) lived for centuries with a belief in God but without a belief in the afterlife. The revelation of God's care and Israel's confidence in divine justice did not automatically demand personal immortality and the possibility of the soul's everlasting blessedness.

Today I am of the opinion that human reason never attains truth—not truth which is life-giving—apart from the mind's being illumined by divine grace. The notion of a purely natural reason sincerely seeking the truth strikes me as an abstraction, for wherever men and women honestly think about life and seek the truth, they must be responding to the prompting of God's Spirit. I also believe that the immortality of the soul cannot be demonstrated by philosophical argument. The only reason for the Christian to insist upon the soul's immortality is the deeply seated conviction that there is a God whose creative purpose cannot be frustrated by injustice or by death. And what is the basis for such confidence? Only our belief in the resurrection of Jesus: "And if Christ has not been raised, our preaching is useless and so is your faith" (1 Corinthians 15:14). If human beings come to believe in an afterlife apart from faith in Jesus, then it may be that the human mind has discerned the logic of hope in the fabric of creation. But the foundation of that hope is the resurrection of Jesus. Again, Origen and Augustine were correct: to believe that the world is created "in the beginning" is to affirm that the logic of creation is disclosed in the life, death, and resurrection of Jesus.

What bearing does this have on the discussion of matter and spirit?

Matter and spirit are not contrary ideas, although they are often juxtaposed. Nor, to be sure, are they identical. If there were no God, then whatever meaningfulness we found in human history or in our existence would have to be invented. We should have to order our world, establish standards of beauty and fairness, and fashion the hopes and vision which would make life worthwhile, at least for thinking men and women. To some degree we are doing this all the time. Yet cultural values are relative, and so are the political, social, and ethical values by which we live. But relative to what? They are relative to some absolute value to which individuals and their societies subscribe, often unconsciously. And what becomes the absolute value? Our nation, perhaps, or our culture, a career, humanity, science, technology, or even history itself. People have, in fact, often reduced the living God into manageable proportions and tried to use God to justify matters of political, economic, or religious taste. Instead of the living God, the absolute value might be the state, the economy, prestige, the human being as such, and so forth. God becomes whatever people serve with their energy and their time, their resources and their loyalty. In short, whenever the creature interprets itself without any reference to the living God, when spirit collapses into matter, then human existence is fundamentally devoid of meaning. Whatever meanings they live by, men and women will have constructed for themselves. And since they are not likely to be at ease with the idea that the only value human life has is the value they attribute to it, people might then formulate a new notion of God which would insure all other meanings, values, and hopes. This is always a dangerous course, because a fabricated notion of God is still idolatrous: the mirror image of every idol is the human being which has tried to deify itself.

But God does exist, we tell ourselves. We are Christians; for us, God is real: "'I am the Alpha and the Omega,' says the Lord God, 'who is, and who was, and who is to come, the Almighty'" (Revelation 1:8). What prevents us, however, from drifting too far toward the next world and undervaluing this one? After all, if we are destined to be with God for all eternity, maybe we should not devote too much time and energy to earthly affairs. A modest amount of food and clothing should be sufficient. There would be little point to composing symphonies and creating works of art, building churches or the hundreds of gadgets technological society manufactures for its convenience. Human existence would appear as a transit lounge, or a valley of tears, or a stepping stone to eternity. The truly wise would have their minds and hearts set on everlasting life. In this view of things, a different notion of God has been constructed. Matter has been collapsed into spirit and God becomes religion, or death (which one awaits daily, not knowing the day or the hour); God becomes merely the sanctuary to which one flees in order to escape the world. The problem involved in this line of thinking is that real human needs could be ignored, or what would be equally tragic, abandoned to the hands of God. The best and brightest people would spend their lives on spiritual quests, like knights searching for the Holy Grail. Human beings would no longer need to exercise their imagination and creativity toward building the earth into a place which reflects divine artistry and justice. Matter, they would believe, is unworthy of God, and they might come to regard the world as the playground of the devil.

Clearly, when matter or spirit is understood too exclusively and our thinking is dominated by one or the other, then the human being disorients itself with respect to God and the world. The formula worked out by the Second Vatican Council attempts to bring the two together. The Christian, in fellowship with men and women of good will everywhere, is committed to building the earth. At the same time, the Christian believes that the ultimate worth of the human being lies not in its technological accomplishments or in the meanings constructed by artists and philosophers, but in its destiny, which is union with God. The Council's Pastoral Constitution on the Church in the Modern World states this explicitly.

Yet, does this formula try to answer the question without meeting the issue? Is it a case of wanting one's cake and eating it too? To position matter and spirit, this world and the next, in tension with each other may respect our experience, but does it settle the underlying theological problem, namely, why does a spiritual God create a material universe?

First of all, I do not know how to define the term "spirit" without referring to the human soul, and the soul, I have suggested, might be defined as that about human beings which is most worth saving. What is most worth saving is human love; love is the properly human contribution to creation. Human beings, obviously, do many things. They eat and sleep, they work and raise children, they laugh and celebrate, and they die. Such activities are not simply another variety of animal behavior, for the human being is also free. And freedom is given so that love might be perfect. Without freedom, properly human love would never exist. Men and women can grow beyond self-centering behavior; they can count the interests of others to be more important than their own; they can learn patience and compassion; they can face the hardness of life without yielding to bitterness and despair; and they can do all this with the knowledge that they are free and that they freely choose to accept the mystery which they are.[5] Human love is worth saving precisely because, in developing its freedom, the human being creates with God something new and wonderful in the universe. As freedom is made perfect, that is, as the power to love is redeemed and made holy, we glimpse why the mystery at the heart of creation is the forming of the human soul. Think of it: love which extends to neighbors, to strangers, to the unlovely, to the unwanted, and to enemies, is free and gracious. It cannot be forced. Love need not be given, as anyone who has struggled to be a lover realizes. Love is the one dimension about human beings which trips the alarm and signals lasting beauty and mystery. Love is another name for spirit, and the presence of love anywhere in our world should make us confident. For in a universe where love is possible, God must reign as the Spirit of love and the source of every life-giving desire.[6]

Human beings will continue to labor, to build, to sacrifice for the future, and to plan better societies. They will continue to write literature, create works of art and music, make scientific breakthroughs and technological advances. And they will do all these things because they are human, flesh and blood, endowed with imagination and intelligence. Yet all these activities remain temporary, that is, conditioned by time and place. Human beings build their monuments of culture, science, art, history, and literature; they fashion societies and governments. These creations, in turn, build us. But do we love music? Do we love our sculptures and paintings, our gardens and cities, our satellites and literature? Do we really love the works of our own hands? I don't believe we do. Yet why do we labor, create, struggle with inspiration, admire genius, and express ourselves? Because, I think, that by doing so human beings become spirit, human beings become ensouled, and freedom is made perfect as love becomes personalized in men and women.

God did not make us pure spirit; rather, God is still creating spirit here and now. The universe of spirit is still emerging from the creative hands of God, from the breath of the Spirit over the formlessness of sin, confusion, injustice, and greed. In other words, to think that God might have worked more economically by creating us immediately as pure spirit fails to understand what spirit is or what it means to create. God is still fashioning the human spirit in ways that will appear to us at once simple and complex: simple, because the creative law is the law of love; complex, because the way human beings learn to obey this law are so intricate, so personal, and so much a part of the sorrow and mistakes, the struggle and work and heroism, the building and letting go, which enter our lives. Matter and spirit are shades of light which help us to see who and what we are. The face of creation changes as darkness is blown aside by the breath of God, or as the Word of God takes flesh in our hearts. Teilhard was correct. Matter has its spiritual side. But in his eagerness to trace a trajectory of divine purpose in evolution itself, Teilhard may have been distracted from the fact that matter has no power of its own to become spirit. The Spirit of God *gives* life and order; matter does not become spirit any more than clay becomes a jar outside the crafting hands of its maker.

Personal Creation and Personal Sin

In his *Confessions,* Augustine remarked on a tendency toward sin even in infants. The child who cries insistently for its needs to be satisfied already shows a trace of that greed which will characterize the pattern of later sin. He wrote:

> It can hardly be right for a child, even at that age, to cry for everything, including things which would harm him; to work himself into a tantrum against people older than himself and not required to obey him; and to try his best to strike and hurt others who know better than he does, including his own parents, when they do not give in to him and refuse to pander to whims which would only do him harm. This shows that, if babies are innocent, it is not for lack of will to do harm, but for lack of strength. . . . Such faults are not small or unimportant, but we are tender-hearted and bear with them because we know that the child will grow out of them. It is clear that they are not mere peccadilloes, because the same faults are intolerable in older persons.[7]

I do not find Augustine's comment particularly attractive because I don't believe he does sufficient justice to human experience. While I would not argue that children are born into a state of pure innocence (pure innocence is an abstraction), I would insist that children are born into very human families. Some parents will rear their children wisely, educating them about manners, morality, and reverence for the Lord. Others will neglect the moral and spiritual upbringing of their children. But human beings are not born good or evil, at least not in a moral sense. They merely are born. Goodness enters into us when there are others around us who love us dearly, for by loving us they love goodness into us. We become good by accepting the goodness of others.

Children are not judged according to the same moral standard by which we judge a teenager, nor can a young boy or girl be judged by the standard which we apply to adults. And the reason is that men and women have to grow into their freedom in the same way that a child has to grow into clothes which are still too large. As we grow into freedom and develop our capacity to give and receive love, then the possibility of doing evil arises. It might be helpful to note that, to some extent, sin is unavoidable, because the clear, unencumbered exercise of freedom is not won without a fight. And the fight is nothing less than the resistance of any created thing to order and form. The soil's resistance to the plow, the clay's resistance to the shape being forced on it by the craftsman's finger, the memory's resistance to exercise, and so on, are metaphors for what is happening in the ensoulment of the human person. But we should not readily pronounce every human inadequacy to be sinful, for much of the behavior which we would identify as sinful, the Creator might simply see as the growth of the creature into the fullness of its freedom and its power to love. Furthermore, a great deal of the spiritual tension we experience arises solely because we have come to know Jesus. If we had never listened to the Sermon on the Mount, if we had never heard Jesus telling us to forgive "seventy times seven times," to love our enemies and to do good to those who might persecute us, not to become anxious over what we are to eat or to wear, and so on, then we would not feel so inadequate in God's presence. The tension or struggle we experience actually ought to reassure us, for this experience confirms that the Spirit of Jesus is making our souls Christian.[8]

It is possible for freedom to develop without one's falling into sin. Jesus grew this way. The more one has been loved and has accepted that love—and accepting love is the key here—the more one's mind and heart will be directed toward loving consistently and regularly doing what pleases God. Most human beings have not been given unrestricted goodness, however: we love one another, but there are limits to the love we are willing or able to give. Furthermore, most of us are neither ready nor willing to let someone love us absolutely and unconditionally. There are too many things of which we are ashamed, too many secret doubts about whether we are truly worthwhile. We alternate between too many moods, and our tendency toward self-pity and pride destablizes our best intentions. On the one hand, we don't offer one another unrestricted love; on the other hand, we would find it hard to accept such a boundless gift. In other words, we do not love each other as God loves us, nor do we leave ourselves fully open to another's love, as a daughter or son of God would. As a result, most human beings have not been set fully free. Freedom is engaged at its deepest level when one human being trusts another, but the ability to do this depends in large measure upon someone else's having trusted us first. In loving someone, I am really trusting that person to accept my love, and my loving enables that person to realize that he or she is worthy of trust. My trusting another enables that person to grow in freedom. The point is elementary. So too in the case of Jesus. Jesus was loved by God unconditionally, in the same way that God cherishes each of us. But Jesus accepted that love, and for our sake it was good that he did. God's love so freed Jesus that he trusted God with his life. And thus through Jesus the rest of us are able to learn what it means to be a son or daughter of God.

It is important to understand that good and evil are not simply opposites. People do indeed sin. We are capable of doing horrible things to one another. But evil is what happens when human freedom fails to develop. Instead of trusting, there is fear; instead of loving, the creature spirals inward and its affection turns increasingly on itself. Thus it takes time for us to become good. Human beings are not made good only to lose, through the process of growing up, their innocence and native beauty. Goodness has to be put on; it must be received.

We help to make one another good by loving our own goodness into others. That is why the soul of an infant is different from the soul of a martyr, or of its parent, or of its teenage brother or sister. In God's sight, of course, each human being is good precisely because divine goodness is responsible for its being created. I often ask a class, "Is something good because you love it, or do you love it because it is good?" The fact is, I think, that we make people good by investing some of our self into them. We fall in love with other men and women as we discover goodness in them. And where did it come from? The goodness we perceive in them comes from those who have loved them before us, love to which they have said yes. And so, every human being is good because God loves us, and God loves us because we are good. Divine goodness is continually being loved into us. In accepting God's love, or anyone's love for that matter, goodness is also being loved or drawn out of us. In loving their child, parents are delighting in their own goodness now embodied in their daughter or son. As the child responds and returns its affection, it reveals the wonder of the truly new creation which every human being is. So too, as human freedom develops and we learn how to put on the love which others would give us, then the full power and direction of creative grace is revealed.

Redemption is not a divine repair work upon a creation that lost its way. Redemption is creative grace; it is creation coming to full term as God works upon our power to trust and to love: to love God, other men and

women, and ourselves. The creature will twist inward
unless constantly pulled by fresh overtures of love from
outside. This is what God does in Jesus. God promises not
to leave us: not simply to remain in our midst, but not to
let us alone, not to let us grow tepid or complacent, not
to let us forget the extent of God's personal love for us,
not to let us gravitate toward the center of our selves.
Always, God prods us outward, away from self-centeredness, away from fear, away from resentment. The fact that
this happens, that it need not happen at all, that there is
little practical or utilitarian value to its happening; the
fact that human freedom continues to pass through fire
and become resplendent in men and women who are real
lovers: this is God's sign that the Spirit is over the world.

Love, freedom, and trust are related. The human being
is not fully developed until it achieves genuine freedom.
But freedom does not blossom apart from trust. Unless one
is willing to trust, one cannot become free. And this is no
accident. Some would prefer to detour around trust and
take a more certain road to authenticity. That is, they want
to be sure that others are absolutely sincere; they want
their love to be grounded upon certitude, not upon trust.
This is not the way freedom grows, however. Freedom
requires that we entrust ourselves to one another if we
want to experience love. Apart from trust there can be no
genuine love, no lasting friendships, for real love is the
fruit of freedom.

Fear blocks freedom. We are afraid to trust God completely, because God is all powerful. If the life of Jesus is
any lesson to us, then we might be afraid to trust God
because we have been scared by the cross. We are afraid
to trust others because they can disappoint us, or, what is
worse, they might reject us. We are afraid to trust ourselves. We know too well how easily our hold upon loy-

alty, patience, and compassion can slip. Fear is just another name for sin, and fear is the enemy of love. We cannot love someone—whether God, other people, or ourselves—of whom we are afraid. Perhaps the basic fear lying at the root of all other fears is our fear of death. Every act of self-surrender, of trust, involves a risk; it is a fore-taste of that final act of surrender which our dying will be. "For the wages of sin is death," Paul wrote. Sin holds us enslaved by keeping us tied to our fears. Why do we lie, except for fear of being uncovered? Why do we harm another, except for fear of losing someone or something? People fear loneliness; they fear being poor or hungry; they are afraid of being laughed at, of being ill or aged, of not having what others have. People are afraid of being loved, really and fully loved, because love tears away our defenses and makes us vulnerable to each other and to God's embrace.

Break the fear of death, therefore, and you destroy the power of sin. "The mind of sinful man is death, but the mind controlled by the Spirit is life and peace." And Paul continued: "For you did not receive a spirit that makes you a slave again to fear, but you received the Spirit of sonship. And by him we cry, 'Abba, Father'" (Romans 8:6, 15). Or to make the same point in different words, God has broken the power of sin by raising Jesus from the dead. By following Jesus, by allowing God to love us in and through Jesus, we encounter the one whom Jesus called "Abba, Father." The route to freedom, Jesus revealed, is trust: love lies at the heart of being human, and to experience the goodness which has been loved into us, God must be trusted. It's as simple as that.

"Do I have a soul worth saving?" The answer is yes, for the soul is that which is of God in me: it is the mystery of love poured into me, love given and received, given by

parents and friends, given by the living God, and gratefully accepted. The soul is my freedom made perfect
because I learned to trust: to trust others, to trust myself,
to trust God. The soul is my love, the small but brilliant
response I have made to my brothers and sisters. This is
the reason for which God is creating me.

To Summarize

The central idea of this chapter has been that the
human soul is constantly being fashioned. All the forces
that stretch and direct human freedom toward greater love
and compassion are the creative energies which form us.
These energies are of one piece with the universe from
which we came, and thus we might say that the material
world, together with the people, places, things, and
events which define it, serves the creation of the human
soul. The chapter opened with a little speculating about
the material universe, for I wanted to indicate the difference between being struck by the fact that the universe
exists and realizing that the universe is created. We may
never know for sure that there was ever a time when matter in some form did not exist, but we do know that the
human spirit can only be created from the possibilities
which material existence offers us. We do know that
beings of flesh and blood are being ensouled as they exercise their capacity for freedom and love. The clue about
creation is given to us in the present, immediate experience each person has of being formed. I also tried to show
that the paired terms—matter and spirit, body and soul—
need to be understood in a way that does not encourage a
flight from the material world or from our responsibility
to make the world ever more human. The human spirit is
fashioned within the conditions of this world: that much

we know. The destiny of the human spirit is union with God and communion with one's sisters and brothers: how materiality will figure into the final state of things is something we do not yet grasp. For the Christian, God's creative purpose does not become fully clear apart from the resurrection of Jesus. In raising Jesus from the dead, God does tell us something further about materiality. God did not merely raise up the soul of Jesus, or the memory of Jesus, or his good works. Jesus' rising in the flesh reveals the deeper possibility which lies at the heart of material, physical, bodily existence.

The second of Kant's questions was, "What ought I to do?" The Christian might answer: I must develop my freedom. I must not allow anyone to usurp that freedom; I have to face my fears, and learn how to forgive, to trust, and to love. Even when I submit to authority, I do so freely, recognizing that I still have to take responsibility for my obedience.

Clearly, it is impossible to discuss the soul without talking about the notions of freedom, love, and trust. Nor is it possible to discuss the soul without inquiring about creation itself. For the human soul—the human person in all his or her graced dimensions—is the ground for maintaining that the physical universe is in fact a creation. We know that God has created the cosmos because we know first that God is creating us.

3

Who Owns the Future?:
A Reflection on the
Resurrection

If there is anything else to life besides living it
we would know, wouldn't we, by something
going on inside, like a loud hum or urgency
or an illumination of our insides day and night?
  —David Ignatow, *Whisper to the Earth*

But why should I lie here longer?
I am not dead yet, though in years,
And the world's way is yet long to go,
And I love the world even in my anger,
And love is a hard thing to outgrow.
  —Robert Penn Warren, *Now And Then*

People spend a great deal of time thinking about the future. We make plans, carve out our careers, dream of buying a house, and so on. Not infrequently, while listening to someone talk about things which are not personally engaging or entertaining (like students listening to a class lecture or churchgoers sitting through a dull sermon), our minds quickly drift to what we are going to do afterward.

While on the way to the store, we think about what we want to buy. While shopping, we are thinking about putting away the groceries and cooking dinner. While cooking, we worry whether our company will enjoy the meal. During dinner, we may be thinking about cleaning up the kitchen. While clearing the table, we may be wondering when the company will go home so we can relax and go to bed. Each of us could relate dozens of examples similar to this one.

The most far-reaching plan most people ever formulate is a twenty or thirty year mortgage on a home. We have other plans and dreams too, such as choosing an occupation; but I have found that people generally make those decisions rather quickly, and that very often those decisions were made for them. Parents or teachers greatly influence the choices young people make. "Why don't you become a doctor?" "You would make a fine lawyer." "You should major in economics and go into business, like your father." By the time many teenagers reach college, they have already settled their future careers. They are hooked by a particular lifestyle, and their projected lifework for the most part will probably involve maintaining, improving, and defending the standard of living they have come to prize. College life is often a matter of working out the details.

The disquieting aspect of thinking in the future is that the future has not yet happened. This means that many of us pass a large number of our waking hours in a world not fully real, regularly living several steps ahead of ourselves. That is, we turn the future into a present moment, at least in our imaginations. But the future we are projecting does not exist.

To whom, then, does the future really belong? In fact, if we spend so much time ahead of ourselves, then what becomes of the present? Thinking toward the future robs the present of its richness. We are less likely to notice and appreciate what we have because we are concerned with what we want, what needs to be done, or what will happen next year. Since none of us can guarantee that he or she will live another hour, let alone another year, futuristic thinking deceives us. We cannot imagine the future without us, but neither can we insure that we shall be part of the future. And so, who owns the future?

Still, aren't there times when we have to look forward to the future, either because we anticipate something joyous or because a present experience pains us terribly? The child's impatience for Christmas morning; the young couple's eagerness for their wedding; the person who dreads going to the hospital and sighs for the relief of being back in the open air; the earnest hope of the poor father who looks forward to a day when his grandchildren will be well educated and well fed; the anxious longing of a mother waiting for the safe return of her child: are these not examples of thinking toward the future? Don't these examples represent the stuff of normal human wishing? Yes, they are samples of human wishing, but these examples do not illustrate what I would call thinking toward the future. Rather, they point to something a bit different. We want times of inconvenience, of sickness, of intense longing, or of sadness and pain, to end quickly. In such instances, we don't so much take refuge in the future as we seek to escape the present. And apart from those cases where death is preferable to agonizing suffering, how many of us have adopted the unhealthy habit of wishing our lives away instead of enduring and tasting the present?

Much of the future is owned by "principalities and powers," the false gods which make their advances and their promises, but which have no means of delivering our dreams. After we reach one goal, another immediately takes its place. We buy a pair of shoes today, and tomorrow we start saving for a coat. We graduate from college and then we want to establish our careers. We have our families and our work under way, and society advises us to think about retirement. The problem is not that people think about the future. The problem is that many of us are frequently controlled by a future which does not come to us as a gift but as an obligation ("you have to do this," "you must save some money and buy that," "you must have the resources to enjoy the good life," "you must fulfill all your potential"), or as a fantasy ("perhaps it's not too late to start another career, to marry another person, to become an athlete"). And when our dreams run aground, we may breed those unfulfilled futures into our children; parents can steal the lives of their children by insisting that the child be and do all the things the parent could not.

Oddly enough, for all our preoccupation about the future, most of our planning and strategies are extremely short-range. We don't often think beyond something else to buy, some errand to run, some hobby to pursue, another movie to see, next summer's vacation, or getting our children through school. Really expansive thinking about the future generally characterizes men and women at the forefront of revolutions, people with plans for a new country or a new society, people who dream of a wholly new way of living. Jesus would have been such a person, and so would Plato or Karl Marx. The people who dreamt America and envisioned the ideals of our nation gave us a future, and perhaps their gift unfortunately spared us the bother of thinking further and fresher than they did. Many of us have settled for dreaming and working less energetically; we have not stretched our dream to encompass the

whole world. In Jesus, God revealed to the world its only
real future. But Jesus' vision does not supplant the necessity for us to think about the kingdom of God. The disciples did not simply inherit Jesus' way of seeing things; he
did not release them from having to contemplate the mystery of God for themselves. Unless Christians are willing
to come to terms with the future, then they will be serving
someone else's vision, content to let others do the real
thinking, meditating, dreaming, and working for them.

Jesus thought toward the future, and that future
belonged to God. In fact, God is the future. Jesus never
intended merely to inform us about the kingdom; he
expected us to be always on the lookout for that treasure
in the field, that pearl of great price, that mystery in the
sprouting seed. Each disciple had to put on God's future,
to think it, to meditate on it, to live it thoroughly. Whenever Christians tire of seeking the kingdom of God in their
midst, then Jesus' vision becomes a utopia, something
from another world which is soothing and consoling, but
terribly unrealistic. Jesus did not create the future; he
received it from God. The future came to Jesus as a gift.
And the kingdom was as much God's grace for Jesus as it
is God's grace for us. The kingdom is God's way of coming
to us in the present, just as God came to Jesus and reigned
in his life. The future "comes," God "comes": we must
not overlook the sheer grace of it, like a brilliant sunset
over the ocean, or the smile that creeps across a child's
face, or the scent of honeysuckle on a summer's night, or
the reassuring trust in a friend's embrace. To say that the
future comes from God is not like saying, for example,
that wine comes from grapes; rather, it is like saying of a
new idea, "it suddenly occurred to me." The coming of
God does not refer to God's moving but to God's self-giv-
ing, as when the prophets say, "The word of the Lord came

to me." Or when the Christian prays, "Thy kingdom come." Now, what does this mean?

Living toward God's future does not force us to become utterly impractical. Christians cannot, and should not, avoid serious engagement with this world. They must work, and procure, and prepare; they hold jobs, they purchase and cook food, they build homes in which to raise their families; they plan cities, try to eliminate disease and poverty, educate their young, repair the plumbing, mow the lawn, and so on. Jesus' words about not worrying would be unrealistic if he intended to keep us from thinking about tomorrow altogether.

There is a difference, however, between thinking about the future as if, by making our plans, we had laid rightful claim to it, and thinking about the future under the realization that God is the one who grants it. I don't mean that God gives us time as empty slots which we can fill with our projects and activities. That is not a future; nor is time merely a sum of hours, months, or years waiting to be filled in. The future, oddly enough, is concrete. It is a dream, yes, and a real possibility. But the future also unfolds now. It empowers the present with new meaning and energy. The future makes the present a moment to be welcomed as it trickles into life's most ordinary corners. Because the future is God's gift, the whole of life now appears as grace.

"Blessed are the eyes which see what you see and the ears which hear what you hear." Blessed indeed, if one really does see, if one really does hear; for what we come to see is the loving closeness of God, what we come to hear is the word from God's nearness. This means that one's honest response to the events and circumstances of life, with all its surprises, its satisfaction, its frustration, its lost opportunities, its memories, with its people and relationships, for time wasted and redeemed, is "Yes!" From what depths of the soul does this word come? What secret does the heart grasp so that it knows for sure that its "Yes!" is not only honestly uttered but also gratefully heard? I think that such a soul has secretly known all along that the very possibility of being able to see and to hear is evidence that to be is to be blessed.

The reign of God happens now, if God's presence (however dimly I perceive it) reaches into the way I think, and work, and speak, and plan. God comes to me from the future and thus the present shows itself as gift. If God reigns, then God's presence is the only thing which needs tending: "Mary has chosen the better part," Jesus said, "and it will not be taken away from her." While it would be unwise to romanticize and spiritualize the most ordinary human activities—from eating and washing, laboring and studying, fixing the sink or changing a tire, to doing laundry and chatting with neighbors, weeding a garden or minding a child—I believe that all these things acquire a different tone for the person who lives in the horizon of grace. For such a person, everything is gift; everything in life "comes" from God.

As I remarked earlier, many people permit someone else to create their future; they settle for merely making plans. Another person presents us with a future into which our decisions will have to fit, and we seldom question this. Even nations do not think very far ahead. The limitation of perspective which afflicts individuals also applies to nations. The ordinary person's dream might extend no farther than purchasing a home and raising a family. Such things are only plans; they do not comprise the future. A nation develops its economy, builds its defenses, and protects its best interests by appropriate political, economic, and social choices. Again, such things are plans or strategies; they do not constitute a national future. Who thinks of the world? Who meditates on the justice and respect which should bind families into a nation and nations into a global community? There is no doubt that capitalists and communists try to think about the future, although at the same time they steal ours. And yet the future as they think of it is not a genuine future. Their tactics for making money, for expanding markets, for concentrating political and economic power in their own hands, are stratagems for laying siege to the future. They do not receive the future as a gift, but in various ways they attempt to grab it. Eventually the future will elude them too. At the end of the day, the world will still find nations competing with each other, poised to fight, sometimes going to war, jealous and self-centered, spending their resources without improving the lot of most people. Ultimately, the future has to be God or it is nothing. Paul wrote to the Colossians: "you have been given fullness in Christ, who is the head over every power and authority (2:10) . . . having disarmed the powers and authorities, he made a public spectacle of them, triumphing over them by the cross (2:15) . . . Since you died with Christ to the basic principles of this world, why, as though you still belonged to it, do you submit to its rules?" (2:20).

The real future is the kingdom of God, God's reigning in human lives. The real future, as opposed to its counterfeits, transforms the present. The real future does not deflect our eyes from the present; it does not allow us to lose ourselves in idle daydreaming, nor does it trap us with concerns and anxieties. No, God's future means being absorbed in seeking and doing what pleases God, as Jesus did. God's future opens into compassion, a sense of belonging to the whole human family. Justice characterizes God's future, and trust. God's future never exploits human weakness, nor does it seek to dominate and control. God's future exists in the man or woman who looks at a stranger and knows, honestly and spontaneously, "There is my brother, there is my sister."[1]

The Resurrection of Jesus:
Learning To See the Future

The doctrine of the resurrection has received considerable attention over the last few years. The Easter stories have been studied and interpreted; their historical accuracy has been defended or called into question by Scripture scholars and theologians.[2] The whole of Christian faith undoubtedly rests upon the Easter event. Whatever we affirm about Jesus' divinity, the incarnation, the Church and its sacraments remains ungrounded unless Jesus was raised from the dead. Whether or not the tomb was really empty (that is, whether it had to be empty for a bodily resurrection to have occurred), how to reconcile the conflicting details about witnesses and apparitions of the risen Jesus, what significance the burial cloth might have for us (if the Shroud of Turin finally proved to be such)—these issues have received extensive discussion. According to some theologians, the resurrection is not an exception to the laws of life and death; their creation theology anticipates such a triumph of grace. The resurrection should not sound strange because it corresponds to humanity's profound hope that the universe has integrity, that injustice will not defeat goodness and mercy, that the poor will have their victory, and that death will not be the universe's final word about the great human achievement of becoming ensouled.

If only there were some simple, compelling proof of Christian claims about Jesus which could permanently satisfy our craving for reassurance, then believing the Gospel might be much easier. The struggle to carry one's cross would remain, but we would be free of the burden of not knowing, of never being sure enough that the Gospel message is truly God's word. And yet, even the first disciples did not witness Jesus' rising from the grave with their own eyes. One could argue, perhaps, that if the disciples really believed that Jesus would rise from the dead, they might have stationed themselves close to the burial site and watched for the proof. But the Gospel accounts report fairly consistently that the disciples were not anticipating a resurrection, for they all register confusion and disappointment after the crucifixion, a failure to recognize the risen Jesus, or downright disbelief. I would conclude, therefore, that the disciples were not much better off than we are, even though they had the advantage of resurrection appearances. They did not receive an all-compelling sign which once and for all dispelled their unbelief and doubt. And unless Jesus occasionally repeated his resurrection appearances, I would say that the disciples lived the remainder of their lives under the power of the Spirit, which was theirs (though not fully theirs), just as we do. Even though we may have experienced some moments of great inner peace and conviction about Christ, those moments generally don't last too long. Tomorrow the ordinariness of faith resumes. We realize that, while we possess the Spirit who empowers our faith, we do not have the Spirit fully, but only as a downpayment toward a future gift.

And so, while I have often envied the first disciples their close human contact with the person of Jesus, I cannot say that they enjoyed a more advantageous position than the rest of us. Apparently, belief did not come easily for them. Easter faith, even for the first disciples, was

Easter *faith,* not Easter certainty. If they did not believe, then they would not see the Easter Jesus. What did Paul do for the rest of his life after his vision on the Damascus road? Did he live off the conviction of having seen the risen Jesus? Judging from the story, Paul's encounter with Jesus did not leave him knowing and certain, but blind and confused. What then was the basis of Paul's faith? Was it an indisputable miracle or the power of the Spirit, which was always a power received in faith? Paul, we should remember, was a believer even before his encounter with Jesus. Otherwise, he could not have seen Jesus at all; Jesus would have been unable to reach him.

The resurrection stories, particularly the episode on the way to Emmaus, seem to reveal that God cannot call us to something which we do not want. It was the disciples' desire that God should have vindicated the life of Jesus, their desire that Jesus should have been the answer to their deepest hopes, which made it possible for Jesus to join them, to reach them, and to rekindle the flame of faith in their hearts. If the two disciples had completely given up, if they had simply abandoned their hope concerning Jesus, then there would never have been an Emmaus story. So too, if Paul had not loved God so strongly, with that sincere, headstrong faith we find leaping from the pages of his letters, then Jesus would not have been able to meet him. Because Paul wanted so much to serve God, Jesus was able to call him to be his apostle. Like Nathanael under the fig tree, Paul had been chosen long before he had been called.

From these examples one can see why the action of grace in human lives often shows itself as the Spirit's awakening us to what we really want. Even when sinners are moved to repent, they do so by putting aside lesser desires for the heart's central desire. The sinner wants conversion, for the sinner (like every human being) wants wholeness, which is God. Following Jesus is the Christian's way of attaining what we truly desire. Jesus awakens us to the desires of which we might be only dimly aware, desires to be and to do something great with our selves. In this awakening, ordinary life, with its commonplace challenges and worries, its relief and its surprise, can appear to be, not just any place, but the very place where the kingdom of God is unfolding for us personally here and now. Kitchens and classrooms, offices and markets, city streets and churches, all assume a rich difference once they are seen as the place where God reaches out to us. Perhaps I am expressing the point too piously. Perhaps I ought to say that these are the places whose inner meaning is created by the word of God as we hear it spoken to us from day to day. Ordinary places and activities become, under God's word, not so much extraordinary as singular. The way of Jesus winds through every place where human beings live and work, love and pray, sit silently and dream.

The resurrection stories also teach us something further. To recognize the risen Jesus, to be able to say "It is the Lord," presupposes faith; even more, it supposes love. People don't always realize how much faith they already have, nor do they suspect that the Spirit has been abiding with them to awaken faith and arouse their hope. Such was the case of the disciples after the crucifixion. They still had faith, but their faith was not yet tried and strong. Fear had temporarily paralyzed them—their fear of death, of failure, of having made a mistake about Jesus. Yet they had *some* faith: "You of little faith," Jesus said, "why did you doubt?" (Matthew 14:31).

Now, if we ask why God insists that we be men and women of faith, I would reply that God does not demand faith in order to work miraculous signs, or in order to have us pass a test of allegiance, or in order to demonstrate that we are worthy of God. Furthermore, our faith in Jesus must translate into something even more than "I believe in you, I believe that you are alive, I believe that you come from God." Faith in Jesus should lead to our doing the same work that Jesus does—the work of God—and that work is to gather men and women into a communion of life and love. Through faith (or through trust, it means the same thing here) freedom is made perfect; apart from trust or faith no human love is worthy of its name. The person who is unable to trust is also unable to be in love with another; the person who is not free cannot love. God places such a high premium on faith for the sake of creating community, since community in the Spirit cannot exist without faith in Jesus. Through his resurrection appearances Jesus strengthened the faith of his disciples. He did not set about confirming them individually in their belief. Rather, Jesus joins them more closely to one another by building up their shared faith in himself; he promises always to be *with them.*

For the disciple, love of God is inevitably linked to community. Faith does not terminate in God, as if in a single object or person. Faith which only gets as far as God remains unfinished. The natural dynamic of faith in God for a Christian leads to the fellowship of believers, and the Easter stories prove it. The risen Jesus rebuilt the community of his disciples; the Spirit of Jesus continues that work among us. Communion of life and love is the sign of God's presence.

We can draw still another lesson from the resurrection scenes.

Love disposes us to recognize other people. Think for a minute of a friend, a brother or sister whom you have not seen in a long time. One afternoon you're strolling along and you catch sight of someone from the back walking with a very familiar gait. The person has the same color hair, and swings his or her arms just as the friend would. Your heart jumps at the possibility that this person might be the one you're thinking of. Love disposes us to see the friend, the loved one, even in total strangers. It makes us look a second time at anyone who shares some of the friend's features, as if other people were carrying the partial likeness of the one whom we love.

So also in the resurrection stories. Love enabled the beloved disciple to see Jesus in the stranger on the shore and to cry out, "It is the Lord!" Love enabled Mary Magdalene to hear the voice of Jesus in the one who appeared to be a gardener. And it was probably love, not merely a surrender to evidence, that elicited from Thomas the prayer, "My Lord and my God." After all, it was Thomas who had said to the rest of the disciples, "Let us also go, that we may die with him" (John 11:16).

This suggests to me that we would not be able to recognize an unknown God, a God who would approach us completely out of the blue. Such a God would be a total stranger, like a name picked randomly from a telephone book. So too with Jesus. We could not recognize an unknown Christ. Perhaps this accounts for why the Christian sees Jesus in any gesture of human love, of forgiveness, of selfless service to others. We instinctively associate certain qualities and actions with the person of Jesus: "That is how Jesus would act . . ." "That is what Jesus would say . . ." "That is how Jesus would have been treated . . ." Love prepares us to notice the characteristics of Jesus in countless others and thereby to recognize him in the world today. "Though you have not seen him, you love him; and even though you do not see him now, you believe in him" (1 Peter 1:8). It is extremely important, therefore, to know what we truly love and to be aware of our deepest desires. Love disposes the eye to see form and beauty, to catch loveliness and personality in the shapes and voices of the lives unfolding around us.

Human beings can learn about God, just as they learn about Jesus. In fact, we must learn about God, and this lesson occupies a great portion of human living. The resurrection helps us to understand that no one sees the risen Jesus who has not in some way already been taught, who has not in some measure already believed, and who does not already love. This might not satisfy those who impatiently look for signs and wonders, who want proof and evidence. But could we make any sense out of a sign from God apart from some faith and love which would dispose us to interpret it? How would we have reacted to the news of an empty tomb or to being told that a dead man was now alive unless, because of our desire and hope, this message spoke to us about Jesus? I used to wonder why the risen Jesus did not simply walk up to Caiaphas, or to the Pharisees, or to Pilate, and demonstrate that he had not been defeated. I think I understand now that Jesus could not have done that; at least, he would not have done so. Such people would have been unable to see *Jesus*. This is clear from the fact that they did not really see him beforehand. Yes, they laid eyes on a man; they heard him speak. But they had not believed, and if the risen Jesus had appeared, they would not have known what they were looking at. The risen Jesus could not appear to them because they had no faith which he might have restored to life, no hope which he might have rekindled, no affection which he might have appealed to. Recall how frightened the disciples were when Jesus walked toward them that night over the water. And Mark added: "They were completely amazed . . . their hearts were hardened" (Mark 6:51–52). Mark might also have repeated what he recorded Jesus to have said in an earlier scene on the lake: "Why are you so afraid? Do you still have no faith?" (Mark 4:40). No wonder, because a Jesus in whom we do not believe is a Jesus whom we would not recognize; a resurrection appearance would serve no purpose. In raising Jesus from the dead, God did not revive his corpse. The risen Jesus was neither a ghost nor a freak, but a brand new creation; to recognize him required faith.

Resurrection as Challenge To Think God's Future

The empty tomb becomes a religious problem because it calls our presuppositions into question. We don't anticipate it; people once buried do not return to life in this world. As a result, some simply deny that the Gospel narrative is accurately reporting an historical fact; others interpret the empty tomb symbolically. Still others lead their lives in a permanent state of skepticism; they follow Jesus' teachings but always doubt the historicity of the Gospel's account of the Easter events. The announcement that a man had emerged from his tomb strikes them as religiously meaningless precisely because it is so exceptional. If every Christian were raised from the dead on the third day after burial, and subsequently appeared to family and friends, they could accept the Gospel story without question. But death is too real and final. The empty tomb seems to be denying the reality of death. As a symbol of hope the empty tomb finds a place in religious imagination, since men and women have to live in the horizon of hope. As a religious fact, however, the empty tomb is unique and, let us face it, implausible.

Among the pictures and illustrations which Carl Sagan included in his book *Cosmos,* there is a chilling series of four representations depicting the last days of the existence of our planet and the sun.[3] As the exhausted sun gradually enlarges, the earth will lose it water, its moisture, and atmosphere. The effect will be every bit as dreadful as a global thermonuclear war. Ironically, a nuclear furnace will finally destroy this planet; the earth will be undone by the same star which first gave it warmth and light.

The prospect of this destruction, which is inevitable, can relativize a great many things. All our efforts to preserve the past by writing histories, protecting works of art, excavating and restoring ancient civilizations, must finally yield to nature's holocaust. Contemplating that fate, even though it won't occur for several billion years, could cripple and defeat some of our wildest, most enthusiastic aspirations about building and renewing the earth.

No one, of course, is going to start shelving present plans because of events that are millions of years away. But it is one thing to say that the end is too far in the distance to be taken seriously and that there is work to be done here and now, and another thing to continue living so completely absorbed by our business that we ignore the ultimately transitory nature of the physical universe. The end of the world, in other words, is also a prospect which calls our presuppositions into question. And because it is so radical a challenge, it can be forgotten, denied, or held in suspension with the pragmatic attitude that life must go on.

For me, the problem about the empty tomb is not whether the account is factual. The empty tomb never really served as proof or convincing sign of the truth of Jesus' life and teachings. Rather, it creates a stumbling block; it causes people to question and re-examine their suppositions about the world, their beliefs, and the grounds of their hope. What advantage is there in knowing that the tomb was empty so long as this knowledge remains only at the level of religious fact? Many people accept the Gospel stories—with all the miracles, events, apparitions, and special effects—as literally true. Yet this does not guarantee that the truth of the Gospel has touched their hearts and turned their minds. The empty tomb does not merely announce, "Jesus is not here." It says further, "He is ahead of you . . . he is risen."

In other words, the resurrection stories lead to a transformed vision of the present world, to a way of finding the Jesus who is ever ahead of us. The empty tomb does not mean that we can avoid death's prison, any more than it denies that someday the earth will exist no more. For those who have the eyes and heart to see it, resurrection is the reality of communion among men and women. It proclaims the possibility of a love that extends beyond gender and nationality, beyond culture and personality. Resurrection testifies to the fact that people who love in this way will be grasped by God and drawn into the timelessness of God's love for Jesus and for all his sisters and brothers.

Our belief in the resurrection of Jesus gives no ground to those who would discount the tragedy and the anguish which many human beings have endured; it does not pretend that the grave can be softened with promises of everlasting blessedness. Resurrection means that the Spirit will raise men and women to life, to life as they may have wanted it without knowing what exactly they are seeking. Perhaps the empty tomb symbolizes a human being set free from fear, set free of alienation, set free from the anxiety of existing alone, set free of the physical constraint which prevents one person from giving himself or herself totally to another. I think the Gospel's report of an empty tomb reflects an historical fact, and this fact challenges us

to reconsider whether we have understood the true nature
of creation. It also challenges the extravagant lengths to
which people go in order to preserve their youth and their
health. The empty tomb does this by revealing that the
way many people are presently living is already a way of
death; many have not discovered what it means to be fully
alive. For the disciple, Jesus is the first one to step into
newness of life, the first human being to be fully created.
In raising Jesus from the dead, God shows the true face of
creation, the mystery and meaning behind the words, "Let
there be light . . . and that light has come into the world
. . . and the darkness has not overcome it." In the resurrection, the world's real future is previewed; in raising
Jesus from the dead, God definitively tells us to whom the
future belongs. The future belongs to the children of God;
they will inherit a new heaven and a new earth.

The New Galilee

The resurrection was not a private event in the life of
Jesus; it was an event which of its nature involved both
Jesus and his disciples.[4] The ascension, which was a distinct though not a separate moment of the paschal mystery, also shows the disciples being drawn into deeper
contact with the God who had been revealed in Jesus. The
risen Jesus has been taken from us, hidden from our sight
by a cloud. Whatever hopes the disciples might have har-
bored for keeping Jesus with them were dramatically
changed by the ascension. Jesus told Mary Magdalene not
to cling to him. Likewise, God was telling all the disciples
through the ascension that they could not have Jesus with
them in the way he used to be.

This was surely a difficult lesson to learn. I know this,
not so much from what the Gospels tell us, but from my

own experience. Letting go of familiar ideas and images of Jesus is hard. We become so accustomed to imagining Jesus in certain ways, watching with an inner eye the stories and events narrated in the Gospels, that we can forget that Jesus has been hidden from view by the cloud of the ascension: "He was taken up before their very eyes, and a cloud hid him from their sight" (Acts 1:9). God was teaching the disciples, I believe, that they had to find Jesus in a brand new way.

"Go and tell my brothers to go to Galilee," Jesus said to the women; "there they will see me" (Matthew 28:10). In Mark, the instruction was given by a young man in a white robe: "He is going ahead of you into Galilee. There you will see him, just as he told you" (Mark 16:7). But where was Galilee, or, rather, where is Galilee now? This question is important for every new generation of Gospel readers. The German Scripture scholar, Willi Marxsen, observed:

> To overstate the case, Mark does not intend to say: Jesus worked in Galilee, but rather: Where Jesus worked, there is Galilee. . . . Galilee is thus Jesus' "home" in a far deeper sense than the merely historical. It is the place where he worked, where—hidden in the proclamation—he is now working, and will work at his Parousia.[5]

Each of us, therefore, has to discover our own Galilee, that place where Jesus always walks ahead of us. For the first disciples, this required facing the world without the Jesus they had known and learning how to touch him again. From now on, however, they would touch him, not with their hands, but with an inner comprehension of how closely Jesus had identified himself with men and women.

How could the disciples find themselves in the company of sinners and outcasts without recalling that Jesus had often kept the same company? How could they walk through villages and not be moved by the beggars at the roadside, the men loitering at streetcorners, women abandoned by their husbands? How could they not feel pity for the ordinary people who obeyed their governors and religious leaders but who had not been taught how to find the living God? How could the disciples meet the poor, the sick, the burdened and oppressed, without remembering how the sight of them moved Jesus, what Jesus would have said or done, or how he took time to listen, to teach, to share a meal? Not only would they recall how Jesus had been so at ease among these people, but as time went on they would understand how Jesus had actually identified with them, his brothers and sisters. In touching them, in seeing them, in serving them, the disciples were touching, seeing, and loving Jesus. They knew this to be so.

Finding Jesus in a new way was one aspect of the ascension. Another aspect was Jesus' commissioning the disciples to be his witnesses. The disciples would go forth from Jerusalem and preach the Gospel to the ends of the earth; this is an obvious way of interpreting the missioning text of Matthew 28:16–20. Jesus surely intended this.

But being a witness to Jesus also suggests something else. Being his witness might mean that the disciples would be the ones who point to Jesus, indicating who and where Jesus is. Thus the disciple looks at the poor, the lonely, the landless, the powerless, the widow, the hungry, and says, "There is Jesus." The one bearing witness to Jesus looks at the refugee, the elderly, the prisoner, the drug addict, the one who knows nothing of God, and testifies, "There is Christ." This kind of witnessing draws attention to two things. First, it identifies Jesus with his sisters and brothers: "Whatever you did for one of the least of these brothers of mine, you did for me" (Matthew 25:40). Second, the disciple bears witness in today's world to those situations in which Jesus is most likely to be found. In his dying, the passion of the world becomes the passion of Jesus. The injustice done to the one is the injustice done to the many. In his rising, the Jesus who suffers for the people now suffers in the people. The injustice done to the many becomes the injustice done to the One.

Bearing witness to Jesus also brings the disciple to pray as Jesus did. When Stephen, as he was being stoned to death, had a vision of Jesus, he made the same prayer that Jesus offered for his enemies as he was dying on the cross: "Lord Jesus, do not lay this sin against them," even as Jesus had prayed, "Father, forgive them, for they do not know what they are doing." When John caught sight of the Lamb and the glorious Christ, he took hope and prayed for himself and his community, "Come, Lord Jesus!" At the Last Supper, knowing that his life was in danger, Jesus prayed to his Father, and he was not in the Father's presence more than a few minutes before he began to pray for his disciples. The Gospel seems to be telling us that Jesus cannot be with God without thinking of those whom he loves, in the same way that most of us are not in Jesus' presence for a few moments before we start thinking prayerfully of those who matter to us. Isn't this what happened when Jesus was praying on the mountain and "saw" his disciples in the boat struggling against the wind and the waves?

To be with God is also to be aware of others, particularly those whom we love and for whom we would naturally pray. But as we grow in the Spirit of Jesus, the circle of those who matter to us widens. We may find ourselves bringing before God people whom we have never met but whose lives have become important to us. We start loving the world as God loves it, with eyes which are wide enough to embrace the whole human race. The disciple bears witness to Jesus' solidarity with all men and women by the kind of prayer he or she makes.

The ascension implies one more thing about the way Christians pray. "Men of Galilee," the angels asked, "why do you stand here looking into the sky?" (Acts 1:11) Men and women of the true Galilee will learn, under the Spirit's tutelage, to find Jesus in the world, in their cities and neighborhoods, in their homes and among their acquaintances. In addition, they will learn that God is not "up there" or "down here." God does not occupy one place: God is everywhere, in all times and places. This should sound fairly obvious. Yet how do we pray? Many of our prayers begin with "Come, Lord," or "Turn your ear to me and listen," or "Reach out to me, Lord, and touch me with your hand." The wording of the prayer conveys the idea that God actually moves, or stretches a hand, or opens eyes and ears, and our minds tell us that such is not the case. It is we who do the moving. In beginning our prayers this way, we are asking, in effect, for God to help us to notice Jesus, to open our eyes toward his presence and movement, to turn our ears to the sound of his word, to be able to feel his presence in our hearts. The language we use tends to spatialize the God who does not move from place to place, and to imagine God as having eyes, ears, and hands. As the author of *The Cloud of Unknowing* suggested, the ascension symbolizes a new mode of Christ's being with us:

> Yes, Christ did ascend upward and from on high sent the Holy Spirit but he rose upward because this was

more appropriate than to descend or to move to left or right. Beyond the superior symbolic value of rising upward, however, the direction of his movement is actually quite incidental to the spiritual reality. For in the realm of the spirit heaven is as near up as it is down, behind as before, to left or to right. The access to heaven is through desire. He who longs to be there really is there in spirit. The path to heaven is measured by desire and not by miles. . . . We need not strain our spirit in all directions to reach heaven, for we dwell there already through love and desire.[6]

We depend upon images in order to focus our imagination and to pray to God as one friend to another. Yet we should also ponder what the ascension reveals. The believer always carries the Spirit within. Every thought, every word or action, every spoken or unspoken intention, every effort to listen attentively to one another, every concern, proceeds from that temple of God which each Christian is, if indeed we are alive to the Spirit. As the believer puts on Christ, growing daily into the image and likeness of God, the Spirit permeates our lives. The steady purifying of our power to love so that it becomes more firmly rooted, less self-conscious or self-centered, more spontaneous and free, proves that our creation is still taking place. To paraphrase the beautiful text of Deuteronomy 30:11–14: The Lord Jesus is no longer in the heavens, that we should be looking for him there. Nor does he live in some distant holy land, that we should have to journey to him there. Jesus does not dwell in some temple or tabernacle, that we should have to spend our time seeking him in a church, nor in the pages of sacred books, that we should need someone to teach us how to find him there. The Lord Jesus is within us—not just within me, but among us. He dwells in our midst, in the minds and hearts of his disciples. To find the Lord one has only to look within and to listen to the sound of one's own desiring. "I want to know God. I want to touch God. I want to experience God's love and I want God's hand to shape my life." Such praying is exactly the sort of prayer we should expect from people in whom the Spirit of God is stirring and praying, with sighs too deep for words (Romans 8:26).

The Easter Christian prays with the whole of his or her life. Men and women fully human and free, rejoicing in the earth's goodness, bearing their humanity with its strengths and weaknesses, delighting in a fine meal or great music, working, recreating, thinking, singing, raising a family, engaged by the hundreds of activities and interests which God made possible by creating us the way we are—these people praise God by being fully themselves. Sometimes they break into the words of an explicit prayer, but it is possible to be praying constantly without always pausing to speak to God. God is praised—and delighted, I think—when men and women do their best at being human. God must surely be gratified when any of us is immersed in the work of building this world and proving ourselves good stewards of whatever God has given us. For the Easter Christian, for the one who is aware of the source and purpose of every good gift, the whole of human life is worship. It is prayer, it is a liturgy which breathes with meaning and faith.

Before leaving these reflections on the resurrection and ascension, I should like to offer one further idea. If our images and concepts about Jesus must pass under the cloud that has hidden him from our sight, as Luke writes, then does the same thing hold true for Jesus' ideas about the Father? In other words, did Jesus at some point in his life have to surrender some of his expectations and his way of thinking about God?

This question can never be definitively answered. It would make sense to me, however, to suggest that Jesus may have had to let go of his own picture of the successful establishment of the kingdom. Jesus had to let God do something in and through him which Jesus, from his standpoint, might have been unable to discern clearly. God had designs on the life of Jesus that went far beyond Jesus' earthly ministry. In fact, the Gospels hint at this. There might well have been an historical turning point in Jesus' life when he realized that his preaching had not sparked the kingdom in the dimensions he had hoped for, and when the road to Jerusalem (and to the cross) emerged into view.

If it is true that each of us must eventually let go of our attempts to define life's meaningfulness and purpose according to our limited perception of success and failure, then perhaps Jesus, as a person of faith, experienced something similar. To define life from our perspective, according to our poor grasp of what is worthwhile and successful, is very understandable. Learning that the human viewpoint is too narrow for grasping what God judges as valuable or worthless belongs to our ongoing creation. We are not guilty of sin, of course, simply because our vision is short-range. In fact, God creates in us eyes that will see farther and discern ever more clearly the true proportions of God's involvement in our lives and in our world. God was creating Jesus each day too, enlarging his grasp of his mission, responding to Jesus' prayer by deepening his contemplative insight and empowering him to guide others along the same road. The resurrection is a letting go in two directions. It is our letting go of the familiar Jesus in order to find him in new and different ways. It is also Jesus' letting go of his ministry among his own people in order that the Father might work through Jesus the divine saving plan for the whole human race.

Adopting a contemplative attitude toward one's own life does not happen easily. And yet, God has designs on each of our lives which extend beyond what we think we are accomplishing. The sympathetic glance which someone noticed, the gesture of friendship that came so easily but which counted for so much to another person, the influence of parents on children, friends on each other, teachers on their students, the powerful example of Christians living their faith—all these converge on that larger scheme of providence that encloses every human life, including the life of Jesus. What God could do through Jesus assumed enormous proportions after he had commended his spirit into his Father's hands. To see one's life contemplatively is to leave oneself open to God's designs, to realize that God works in and through all of us, as God did (and continues to do) through Jesus. We are witnesses to all of this. We witness to the fact that the future belongs to God—my future, your future, Jesus' future too: God owns it all.

Conclusion

As we get older, we may find ourselves asking fewer questions about life and faith, but the ones we raise are more likely to be worth asking. The matured human being no longer holds an opinion about every topic under the sun, and when judgments have to be made, they are made cautiously and humbly. The life of the mind passes through its seasons. Having made mistakes, the adult has learned to tolerate differences—different viewpoints, different ways of saying the same thing, different styles of living and worshiping. For, while people are obviously different, wisdom teaches us how to identify that common thread which runs through so many lives both within and outside our religious tradition, namely, the desire to love and serve God above everything else. No one gains religious understanding without undergoing the discipline of wisdom; the mind is made patient by the things it suffers. The mind makes mistakes. It presumes in its youthfulness that more can be known, and known certainly, than it is capable of understanding. The mind takes a long time to put on an idea, and after it has clothed itself several times with ideas which are more stylish than correct, which prejudice its search for truth, or which have foolishly driven a wedge into friendship, the mind feels its need for the healing grace of God's word. Wisdom chastens the mind by letting it discover that the mind is truth's hand-maid, never its master and never to be confused with truth itself.

But coming to the truth has its joyous side too. When truth seizes the mind, the mind experiences the refreshing release and freedom which come from sharing in the life of another. It is like listening to someone reveal her deep-est thoughts and being overcome with reverence because we have been given access to another's soul. Coming to the truth, which the Christian realizes is a coming into God, is the grace and privilege of knowing the world, at least in some very small way, as God knows it. The Chris-tian who stands in the truth discovers that he still does not know the Father, but that he does know Jesus and that Jesus has been placing him, piece by piece, in the Father's presence.

As we get older, knowledge also simplifies. We devise little formulas or shorthand expressions which condense, very economically, what it has taken years to learn. A phrase suffices where once we spoke in paragraphs; a sim-ple word abbreviates entire sentences. Yet such simplicity is deceiving. Precisely how deceptive brevity of expres-sion is becomes clear whenever we proceed to introduce another to Christian faith. There are no short-cuts to gen-uine religious understanding. Although a prudent teacher can guide us through thickets of useless information and irrelevant questions, and a believer more seasoned in the Spirit can assist us in learning the ways of God, no one can make the journey of faith in our stead. Nor should we let anyone try.

Understanding aims at simplicity, at compression of language, but it does not substitute ideas for experience. John's brief definition "God is love" expressed everything

John wanted to say, but it probably does not represent the fullness of Christian understanding in the minds of all his readers. This kind of comprehension results only from spending one's life in Jesus' company. The straightforward questions and answers in our old catechisms stated admirably and concisely all the Christian needed to believe. But if the Church has relearned any lesson in the twentieth century, surely it is that Christian instruction has to be accompanied by a growing personal relationship with Jesus and that men and women have to be instructed—catechized—about how to initiate and develop that relationship if they are going to understand anything else about Christian faith.

Scripture, like the catechism, often abbreviates. This would suggest that much of Scripture could only have been written by people who had matured in faith; but this should also remind us that only those who have made some progress along the way of faith will fully appreciate what the biblical writers have left us. The evangelists, for example, might not have been eyewitnesses to the things they recorded, but they certainly lived as disciples and friends of Jesus. The Gospels which they wrote capture and reflect a richness of experience and insight which keep stretching their language to its limits. The catechism imparted information and religious formulas, but its simplicity was misleading. People did not necessarily know their faith well just because they could answer the catechism's questions, nor do they necessarily understand their faith any better because they hear and read Scripture. Questions are helpful only when they are truly one's own questions, that is, when they frame the doubts, the hesitations, and the searching which correspond to one's personal experience. Sometimes a community, another person, or a book can uncover our deepest questions for us;

most of us need to be helped in our attempts to interpret our own lives.

In the last three chapters we pursued three direct, though admittedly borrowed questions. They provided the skeleton for a brief catechetical inquiry. "What can I know?" I can know Jesus. I can know the Jesus who even now teaches, heals, rescues, corrects, and loves those who consent to follow him as disciples. I can come into contact with the living God and I can know myself as one who feels his or her inadequacy when surrounded by the divine holiness. But I can also know that God knows me thoroughly, for Jesus has unlocked my inner self to the loving eye of the one he called "Abba, Father."

"What should I do?" I should become fully human and fully free. This I do by following Jesus. In being-with-Jesus, I allow God to ensoul me. Specifically, there are many things which the Christian ought to do. But the Christian will be drawn to do those things, almost naturally, because no one lives in Jesus' company without putting on his mind and heart. Generally, I have to learn how to trust myself, other men and women, and God. The fact that I can love and forgive means that I must assume responsibility for this gift. I must place in God's hands a soul that is worth saving. At the end of my life, with Jesus, I shall commend my spirit into the hands of God.

"What may I hope for?" I may hope that the God who has begun the good work of creation will bring it to completion. I hear the story of Jesus' resurrection and know it to be true, not only because I trust the pedigree of Christian hope, nor only because Easter faith has sustained men and women for so many centuries. I know the story to be true because the capacity to love and to forgive is the only thing which confers significance and purpose on human existence, and in a world where love and forgiveness occur, the power of death has already met its match and begun to yield. If love can break fear, then perfect love breaks into the future. I may hope that human ensoulment will not be lost in the bleak silence of cosmic night. I also know the resurrection story to be true because from time to time the future rushes into the present with its news that the world is different from the way it appears. Behind the ordinariness of daily living—the familiar streets and buildings and rooms, the familiar people and sounds, the routine work and worries—my eye catches the flash of mystery: God is passing through creation, listening to its music, sharing its pain, picking up and holding its beauty. The resurrection is the great Christian story, remembered and retold, about the eighth day of creation. In creating Jesus and raising him from the dead, God answered the question of what we may hope for.

Appendix:
Catholic and Christian

For God, that was too great to be holden even of everywhere and forever, had bound Himself into the narrow room of here and now. He that was in all things had, for pity, prisoned Himself in flesh and in simple bread. He that thought winds, waters and stars, had made of Himself a dying man (H. F. M. Prescott, *The Man on a Donkey*).

Because you are sons, God sent the Spirit of his Son into our hearts, the Spirit who calls out, "*Abba*, Father" (Galatians 4:6).

Two questions which some Catholics have been asking themselves in recent years are what distinguishes a Catholic from other Christians, and what distinguishes Christians from believers of the other major world religions. The first question is prompted, first, by developments which have occurred in the Catholic Church since the Second Vatican Council (1962–1965), and, second, by the Catholic community's increased sensitivity to ecumenism and religious dialogue. The modern Church undoubtedly enjoys a clearer perspective on the political and religious turmoil of the sixteenth century than the theologians and bishops who met at Trent. Today we are able to see that the reformers were often speaking and writing of changes which ought to have been made by the Church but which the Church refused to permit because of human stubbornness, misunderstanding, or fear. The Second Vatican Council, not the Council of Trent, was the Catholic community's authentic response to the Protestant Reformation, at least in a number of important areas. Liturgically, spiritually, and theologically, the reforms initiated by Vatican II would have satisfied many a reformer's desire for a revitalized Christianity. Luther's doctrine of justification, for instance, has been given a far more positive interpretation by Catholic theologians today than four hundred years ago. Liturgy in the vernacular, Communion under both kinds, the availability of Scripture to ordinary people, biblically informed preaching, sacramental rites which people can understand—these are some of the changes brought about by Vatican II which the reformers wanted in the sixteenth century. Many Catholics are sufficiently aware of the new level of understanding among various Christian churches as to raise the question: What now distinguishes us as Catholics from the Protestants? Karl Rahner described the situation this way:

> Everywhere there is a growing understanding of the need for ecumenism. In such a situation it is certainly no longer easy to regard one of the Christian confessions and churches, to the exclusion of all the others, as the only legitimate one and the only route to salvation. . . . The title "Church" is given on all sides, the universal validity of baptism is stressed, there is a recognition of the genuine religious value of many doctrines, institutions, and forms of spirituality in the

various churches, rejoicing at the identity of holy scripture throughout the Christian world, and so on. However, these very attempts at ecumenical rapprochement have made it much more difficult in practice, at least for Catholic Christians, to still allow their Church the unique status which, even at the Second Vatican Council, it claimed for itself as opposed to all the other Christian churches.[1]

The second question is also prompted by events which have taken place in Christian churches over the past two decades or so. Many of us have heard about young people giving up their Christian religion and traveling to the East in order to discover the spiritual treasures of Oriental religions like Buddhism and Hinduism. Even in our own country we have seen the arrival of various cults which attract those who have given up on Christianity because they find it spiritually empty or religiously unsatisfying. Although it may be difficult to take such cults and movements seriously, the issue they often raise is this: There are many roads to the one God, they say. What difference does it make, therefore, which road one takes so long as one arrives at God? This line of thinking, in effect, reduces all religions to a number of ways or paths to the one God and relativizes each of them in terms of a common goal. Now, there is certainly an advantage to passing over into another religious tradition and back to one's own, as John S. Dunne has explained so well in his book *The Way of All the Earth* (1972). Such "passing over" can result in a sympathetic understanding of another religion and an enriched appreciation of one's own tradition. But we still have to ask whether there is something distinctive, indeed something compelling about Christianity which would make it more than just another path to the Absolute, to enlightenment, to Allah, to Yahweh, to the One, to God.

Both questions have been addressed in recent years by Catholic writers, particularly by the Swiss theologian Hans Küng in his book *On Being a Christian* (1976) and by the German theologian Karl Rahner in his book *The Foundations of Christian Faith* (1978). What is remarkable about these works, and what characterizes to some degree the present state of Christian truth in the minds of many Catholics, is the centrality of the person of Jesus (which should hardly be surprising) and the relative disinterest in a number of well-known Catholic doctrines. For there was a time when we distinguished ourselves from other Christians by our belief in purgatory, for instance, or indulgences, or papal infallibility, or the Marian doctrines (virgin birth, immaculate conception, and assumption), or especially the real presence of Christ in the Eucharist. There were also our practices of communal piety, such as the nine first Fridays, benediction, the rosary, novenas, the stations of the cross, meatless Fridays, or fasting before Communion. But when it came to major points of faith such as the divinity of Christ, the inspiration of the Bible, Trinity, incarnation, resurrection, and the presence of the Spirit in the Church, we discovered that here we shared these beliefs with many others who were not Catholic. To anyone who had taken time to think about it, often what divided us was less significant religiously than what united us. But because of other factors such as the suspicion and hostility Catholics frequently faced in this country from non-Catholics, the differences between the churches hardened around loyalties and identities which had social, ethnic, political, and economic roots. Apart from being assured that Catholics had a more complete grasp of apostolic faith than Protestants, my early fears of Protestants

had little to do with Protestant beliefs but a lot to do with
Catholic authorities telling me that Protestants were
opposed to our political and economic advancement.
According to my youthful impressions, Catholics were
also more likely to be Democrats and less likely to be
wealthy.

Of course, if any had thought about the matter further, then it might have dawned on them that the Spirit of
Jesus cannot be fully present in the Church if religion
leads into stereotyping others, if it leads to suspicion and
resentment of others who also claim the name Christian.
In such a case, one's Christianity would no longer be the
religion of Jesus. It would have degenerated into a mere
cult of the transcendent, lacking any real, practical reference to the person of God's Son, Jesus of Nazareth. The
Christian attitude toward and treatment of the Jews
throughout much of our history should underscore the
fact that, in many instances, because of their jealousy and
hatred local churches had ceased belonging to the communion of life and love which alone marks Jesus' true
disciples.

At any rate, it becomes clear that however important
certain teachings have been to us as Catholics, however
much they contribute to our personal and communal identity, these are meaningless unless we share an inner life
which makes us Jesus' followers in a real, practical,
observable way. That helps to explain why Catholic writers today have been drawing careful attention to the personal dimension of Christian faith. For this dimension
involves discovering and following Jesus, coming to know
Jesus (which is more than knowing about him), developing styles of personal and communal prayer, and living the
Gospel's call to witness to Jesus by serving others, by loving, by working on behalf of justice. It is not that other

doctrines are incorrect or unimportant. But not every belief really bears upon our personal transformation; not every teaching we hold as right and Christian actually works for us to make us holy. We believe, for example, that Mary was conceived without original sin. Yet there are probably only a few who appreciate the full significance of that teaching. Since most of us have not integrated this belief into our Christian living (and I am not so sure it can be), one has to conclude that the doctrine of the immaculate conception, for instance, does not make people holy in the same way that following Jesus does.

Following Jesus is a way of declaring that Jesus is Lord. We can speculate about the meaning of his being divine, about how Jesus is related to the Father; we might eventually grasp what is meant by the classical expression "hypostatic union." Indeed, it is important for Christians to know that Jesus is God's Son. But that knowledge is not revealed for the sake of entertaining our minds with a brilliant speculative idea. That knowledge is important for the sake of our living. After all, there is no compelling reason for following Jesus, for imitating Jesus, for judging oneself according to his teaching, for throwing our arms around Jesus as we would around no one else (as Rahner put it), unless Jesus really is God's word to us made flesh and unless it is possible for flesh and blood like us to become real daughters and sons of God.

There are people who say that Jesus is divine but who follow another Lord. In what sense can they claim to be either Christian or Catholic? Their Lord might be prestige, a career, a corporation, their nation, their race, a political party; it might be the Church, their professional class, or any one of the hundreds of things to which men and women give their allegiance. Yet none of these things is Jesus, and so there are people who profess to be Christian but who do not really, practically, lovingly believe in the divinity of Christ. Otherwise, they would not be following something else. Jesus urged his followers not to worry about what they were to eat or to wear. He was not advocating that they stop working and providing for their families. Rather, they were not to *set their hearts on* food and clothes (and presumably other things also) as the unbelievers—"the nations of the world"—do. Doesn't Jesus directly challenge us about the amount of time we spend planning and scheming to make money? Doesn't Jesus expose the hollow loyalty of professing to follow him while giving blind obedience to the profit motive? Jesus warned his listeners that they could not serve both God and money, or God and Caesar. Only one Lord could reign over the whole of a person's life, and to serve Caesar was to dishonor Christ. The "render to Caesar" eventually becomes "we have no king but Caesar." Today, capitalists and communists alike carry the coin of false tribute in their pockets.

The first characteristic, then, of being Catholic (as it would be for every Christian) is that we recognize Jesus as our only Lord. It is Jesus whom we learn to see in others and others whom we learn to see in Jesus. Jesus is the one person above all others whom we listen to and serve. In loving Jesus we discover that other men and women are truly our sisters and brothers. In coming to know and love our brothers and sisters, we come to be known and loved by Jesus.

Being Catholic also defines a manner of living. It involves a special way of imaging the world, of relating to other believers, of expressing our relationship to God. This particular way of viewing life has been incorporated, in more or less pronounced terms, in the work of a number of Catholic writers. One thinks of Sigrid Undset's *Kris-*

tin Lavransdatter, José Maria Gironella's *The Cypresses Believe in God,* the novels and short stories of Flannery O'Connor, Graham Greene's *The Power and the Glory,* and so on. Along a more analytical vein, one might think of Rosemary Haughton's insightful study *The Catholic Thing* (1979). Being Catholic draws one into a universe of symbol and story, of theology and outlook, which is a comprehensive style of being human. It includes a rhythm of life and death, of people fallen but becoming redeemed, of betrayal, purgation, and forgiveness. It is composed of the Catholic tradition's ritual and faith, the conviction that whatever God has made is good, the intricacies and sureness of grace, a glimpse of that providential scheme which somehow embraces each of us, rich and poor, sinner and saint alike. Through the complicated mazes of human weakness, misfortune, and suffering, the human being eventually comes to be redeemed. And even if life does not reach a happy ending, at least it comes to wisdom, self-acceptance, and a measure of hope. The priest bending over the body of a hardened criminal to administer the final sacramental anointing is a great Catholic picture. It testifies to the pastoral experience that even the most confirmed sinner could, in the final seconds of life, be touched by God's grace.

It is largely by seeing the community's faith in action, as people actually live in and because of that faith, that one understands the Catholic identity. This identity should not be reduced to a list of beliefs and religious practices, since life is much larger than our words and rites will ever express. The Catholic Church celebrates life, with all life's moments of tenderness and tragedy, of birth and love, of human work and dreams, of death and new hope. It will bless nearly everything that human beings touch, use, or hold dear because it believes that by blessing created things the believing community uncovers to the eyes of faith the unseen hand of the God who touches, molds, and thereby makes good everything in creation. Just as families have their ways of doing things, their ways of addressing one another, their knowledge of each other's strengths and weaknesses, so too does each Christian church. One has to live with a family for a while to learn from inside and appreciate how the mother is called "mom," or "ma," or "mother"; how the father is called "dad," "father," or "pop"; how the children kiss each other or surprise each other or tease each other; what the favorite meals are, the style of sharing, the way of making beds, and so on into a hundred things which shape a family's character. Being Catholic, I think, is something one appreciates best from inside. Why do we think the way we do, why the liturgy and the kind of prayers, why the centrality of the Eucharist, the fondness for blessing things, the secrecy surrounding confession, the odd contrast between working for the poor and building cathedrals, between collecting food for the hungry and patronizing art, music, and learning? These things only make sense "in the family," as it were, and without that family sense it becomes difficult to explain what the Catholic identity means.

The intuition underlying the Catholic sense of things is nothing other than a rich, penetrating grasp of the incarnation. There is a particular religious aesthetic which corresponds to being Catholic, a way of relating to the world and to God which is based on the belief that through the Word's becoming flesh, every created reality needs to be seen within the new and radiant vision of God's glory. Even our way of relating to God has been transformed by the fact that, in Jesus, God has become a participant in human history, has shared human experience, and forever belongs to the human family as the example of what being fully human and fully religious means. In other words, the doctrinal basis of the Catholic identity is more likely to be the incarnation than any other doctrine. This is quite evident throughout the writings of Karl Rahner and in Hans Urs von Balthasar's multi-volumed work *Herrlichkeit,* which has begun to appear in English under the title *The Glory of the Lord* (1982). Yet the Catholic perspective on the incarnation is not so much that through the whole of Jesus' life God's word was taking flesh (it is certainly that). Rather, the perspective governing the Catholic sense has been for the most part, I think, the wonder or miracle of it all, namely, that God has joined material creation by becoming part of the physical fabric of space and time. Created things necessarily assume a different light when illumined by the holiness of God's incarnate word.

There should be no surprise, therefore, that the Catholic possesses such high regard for earthly things. Family and friendships, human work and human artistry, imagination and intelligence, meal taking and journeying, laughter and learning—all things are sacramental. Through such events God comes. In such events the Catholic believes that people can know, as well as one can in this life, the presence of God. Because of the incarnation, any moment in a person's life can be a graced moment, brimming with meaning for those who have the eyes of faith.

Being Catholic, therefore, shows itself in two important ways. First, it involves a practical discipleship, a way of thinking and behaving which leaves no doubt that Jesus alone is Lord. This is what makes us Christian. Second, being Catholic also consists of a sacramental way of looking at reality. It is a way of focusing and evaluating the

world which takes the incarnation as the truth which symbolically transforms all human experience.

The second question I cited is about our identity as
Christians. Are the various world religions simply different
routes to the one God? Does it make any difference which
religion one belongs to?

I think the Christian should start by acknowledging
that God's grace is wider than Christianity, and, in fact,
that the grace of Christ is wider than the Church. There
are people who remain all their lives marginal church
members. Wolfhart Pannenberg refers to them as "church-
less Christians."[2] They would call themselves Christian in
a broad sense, since they do believe in God and the teachings of Jesus. They may have a more or less precisely defin-
able experience of God. They do not have that deep, personal experience of Jesus which would lead them to know
Jesus clearly and directly as Lord. They do not find themselves drawn into the company of believers, since their
experience of being with Jesus is not fully defined. Nevertheless, in a wide sense they are Christian and eventually
they make their way to God. Some of them may be leading
holy lives. My point is simply that we cannot pre-judge
people and that we have to leave God free to meet men
and women in less than ideal ways. After all, even with
Christianity's emphasis on community, we recognize the
place of the solitary Christian, like the Carthusian, in the
Church. Indeed, sometimes the solitary person has a live-
lier sense of real communion with others, precisely
because of his or her being with Christ, than those of us
who are physically part of communities but who do not
reflect regularly on the holy mystery which binds us
together.

As we enlarge our perception of the manifold and
often complex ways in which God meets human beings,

therefore, we appreciate that people do in fact find God without knowing Jesus. This is not to say, however, that they experience God in the same way that those who are with Jesus do. By the idea of being-with-Jesus, I do not mean being geographically with Jesus, or physically with Jesus, except perhaps through imagination. Being-with-Jesus refers to a manner of thinking, of acting, of loving, of relating to others, of viewing the world. It is a way of talking about our willingness to follow Jesus, to be drawn by his example, to learn from him, and to have our loyalties corrected and shaped by his.

The disciples realized that after being in Jesus' company they had come to think about and experience God differently. God for them could not be the same before and after their time with Jesus, and from then on their experience of God was intimately tied up with their being with Jesus. For the disciples, God came to be the God who is Father of their Lord, Jesus—the one whom God personally chose and anointed with the Spirit, Jesus the Christ. The full force of this new experience, which centered on Jesus' dying and rising and the profound effect this made on the disciples, came when the disciples too were anointed with the Spirit. For the same Spirit which was with Jesus was also, because of him, with the disciples. That Spirit enabled them to know God as Jesus had and to call God their "Abba," or dearest Father. The God who was the Father of Jesus was now their God too.

This is an extremely important point. "Abba" was not merely another title for God. It was not simply the correct name for calling upon God, nor did it reveal, as Bernard Cooke has pointed out, a masculine, patriarchal (and thus religiously limited) understanding of God.[3] "Father" was an abbreviation for the entire range of Jesus' religious experience. To understand that word is to understand the basis of Jesus' teaching, the confidence out of which he preached, the power which enabled him to work miracles and to forgive sin, the love for which he would lay down his life. After all, Jesus died because he loved God. The God he knew was so overwhelmingly the God of mercy and grace that Jesus would die rather than stop preaching what he knew to be true. In the end, Jesus was crucified because he would not change his message; he would not deny his experience of God.

Indeed, Jesus died for us. I take this to mean that Jesus wanted others to know God as he did precisely because Jesus loved people like us. Jesus loved his disciples—he loved Andrew, and John, and Simon, and Peter, and all the others who were his close friends. Jesus cared for the people of Israel. He wanted them to learn how to open themselves to the Spirit and to experience God in a new way. What may not have been immediately or sufficiently clear to Jesus was the degree to which this new experience of God would depend upon men and women being-with-him.

The disciples, of course, were believers long before they started to follow Jesus. Paul, for instance, was a man of zealous faith. He knew how to pray, he chanted the psalms, he read Scripture. Paul knew God even before the event on the Damascus road. So too with James and Thomas, Matthew and Philip, Mary Magdalene, Martha, and the others. We must not think that Jesus merely supplied them with new teaching or new information about God. Jesus made a different experience of God possible, and God was making that experience contingent upon their knowing and loving Jesus.

And so, in asking about our Christian identity, we realize, first, that other men and women know God apart from Jesus. Yet so also did the first disciples. But knowing God in Jesus remains, for us, a very different religious possibility. The God who is Father of the Lord Jesus Christ is not known, in this way and with all that this means, to people of the Jewish faith, or to Buddhists, or to Moslems, or to Hindus. Experiencing God in Jesus is not reducible to the experience of God within any other religious tradition.

Instead of attempting to situate other religions with respect to ours and judging them more or less adequate in comparison with our truth, we should, I think, be trusting that our experience of God is something worth sharing. For this experience has its own power of attraction and this attractiveness is nothing less than an experience of the grace of Christ. Whenever religions are judged in terms of what they teach, their moral principles, what they say (or do not say) about God, then questions about religious identity will be answered in terms which are too theoretical, too intellectual to be spiritually nourishing. The basic question about religious identity should lead us to think about the distinctive nature of people's experience of God. And for Christians, this means considering who God is for us as a result of our being-with-Jesus, whom we also call God's Son.

Being Christian, then, not only requires following Jesus as disciples whose loyalty to the Gospel is unambiguous. To be Christian is also to be drawn into the distinctiveness of Jesus' experience of God.

Notes

Introduction

1. Immanuel Kant, *The Critique of Pure Reason,* trans. F. Max Miller (London: Macmillan & Co., 1881), p. 697. In his book *Fundamental Theology* (New York: Paulist Press, 1981), Gerald O'Collins frequently resorts to Kant's three questions as a way of organizing various levels of his theological reflection. I am indebted to Fr. O'Collins for this clue in arranging some of the material here.

2. Apart from the text of Philippians 2:6–8 (which is quoted in Chapter One), all scriptural texts are taken from the New International Version of the Bible.

3. For a contemporary approach to the doctrine of original sin, see James Gaffney, *Sin Reconsidered* (New York: Paulist Press, 1983), pp. 45–52; Jerome Murphy-O'Connor, *Becoming Human Together* (Wilmington: Michael Glazier, 1982), pp. 89–105, 174–197; Brian O. McDermott, "Original Sin: Recent Developments," *Theological Studies* 38:3 (1977), 478–512. On the theology of baptism, see Aidan Kavanagh, *The Shape of Baptism* (New York: Pueblo Publishing Co., 1978).

4. See Gerald O'Collins, *Interpreting Jesus* (New York: Paulist Press, 1983), pp. 149ff.

5. The notion of a hierarchy of truths is important for dogmatic theology and for spirituality, but its significance for spirituality (as far as I know) has yet to be worked out. The major

Vatican II text appears in the Decree on Ecumenism, #11: "Furthermore, Catholic theologians engaged in ecumenical dialogue, while standing fast by the teaching of the Church and searching together with their separated brethren into the divine mysteries, should act with love for truth, with charity, and with humility. When comparing doctrines, they should remember that in Catholic teaching there exists an order or 'hierarchy' of truths, since they vary in their relationship to the foundation of Christian faith" (Walter M. Abbott, ed., *The Documents of Vatican II* [New York: Herder & Herder, 1966], p. 354). See Avery Dulles, *The Resilient Church* (New York: Doubleday & Co., 1977), pp. 55–58; and Dulles, *A Church To Believe In* (New York: Crossroad Publishing Co., 1982), p. 148, n. 36.

6. While I do not know of a history of theological direction available in English, the reader might want to consult *Writings on Spiritual Direction by Great Christian Masters,* ed. Jerome M. Neufelder and Mary C. Coelho (New York: Seabury Press, 1982); and Kenneth Leech, *Soul Friend: The Practice of Christian Spirituality* (San Francisco: Harper & Row, 1980), pp. 34–89. Also, see William A. Barry and William J. Connolly, *The Practice of Spiritual Direction* (New York: Seabury Press, 1982).

7. On the category of experience in theology, see Gerald O'Collins, *Fundamental Theology* (New York: Paulist Press, 1981), pp. 32–52. Also, Edward Schillebeeckx, *Christ: The Experience of Jesus as Lord* (New York: Seabury Press, 1980), pp. 29–64.

8. See Sharafuddin Maneri, *The Hundred Letters,* trans. Paul Jackson (New York: Paulist Press, 1980), pp. 201–203.

9. On Jesus' "Abba experience," see Bernard Cooke, "Non-Patriarchal Salvation," *Horizons* 10.1 (1983), 22–31; Edward Schillebeeckx, *Jesus: An Experiment in Christology,* trans. Hubert Hoskins (New York: Seabury Press, 1979), pp. 256–71; James D.G. Dunn, *Jesus and the Spirit* (Philadelphia: Westminster Press, 1975), pp. 15–40.

10. On the place of the humanity of Christ in mystical prayer, see William Johnston, *The Still Point: Reflections on Zen and Christian Mysticism* (New York: Fordham University Press, 1970; 1982), pp. 151–170.

11. Two books by Sebastian Moore should be recommended here: *The Crucified Jesus Is No Stranger* (New York: Seabury Press, 1977) and *The Fire and the Rose Are One* (New York: Seabury Press, 1980).

12. On the so-called "negative knowledge of God," see Harvey D. Egan, "Christian Apophatic and Kataphatic Mysticisms," *Theological Studies* 39:3 (1978), 399–426; and his book, *Christian Mysticism* (New York: Pueblo Publishing Co., 1984).

13. Thomas Verner Moore, *The Life of Man with God* (New York: Harcourt, Brace & Co., 1956), pp. 305–306.

14. See Johannes B. Metz, *Poverty of Spirit,* trans. John Drury (New York: Paulist Press, 1968), and William Reiser, *Into the Needle's Eye* (Notre Dame, Ind.: Ave Maria Press, 1984).

15. Dorothy Day, *The Long Loneliness* (San Francisco: Harper & Row, 1952; 1981), p. 139.

16. See John S. Dunne, *The Way of All the Earth: Experiments in Truth and Religion* (Notre Dame, Indiana: University of Notre Dame Press, 1972).

17. A sampling of their writings would include: Panikkar, *The Unknown Christ of Hinduism* (Maryknoll, N.Y.: Orbis Books, 1984 [revised edition]); Rahner, "Christianity and the Non-Christian Religions," *Theological Investigations,* Volume 5, trans. Karl-H. Kruger (Baltimore: Helicon Press, 1966), pp. 115–134; Merton, *The Asian Journal* (New York: New Directions, 1973); and Griffiths, *Return to the Center* (Springfield, Ill.: Templegate Publishers, 1977). The growing importance of the world religions for Christian theology and spirituality can be gauged from works like the following: Paul Clasper, *Eastern Paths and the Christian Way* (Orbis Books, 1980); S.J. Samartha, *Courage for Dialogue: Ecumenical Issues in Inter-Religious Relationships* (Orbis, 1982); Alan Race, *Christians and*

Religious Pluralism: Patterns in the Christian Theology of Religions (Orbis Books, 1982); William Johnston, *The Inner Eye of Love* (San Francisco: Harper & Row, 1978).
18. Karl Rahner, "Thoughts on the Possibility of Belief Today," *Theological Investigations,* Volume 5, p. 21.

1. The Changing Face of Jesus

1. See, for example, Jon Sobrino, *Christology at the Crossroads,* trans. John Drury (Maryknoll, N.Y.: Orbis Books, 1978); Leonardo Boff, *Jesus Christ Liberator* (Orbis Books, 1978); and José Míguez Bonino, ed., *Faces of Jesus: Latin American Christologies,* trans. Robert Barr (Orbis Books, 1984).

2. The major work is still Raimundo Panikkar's *The Unknown Christ of Hinduism.* Much work remains to be done for presenting an understanding of Jesus which reflects the religious and cultural pluralism of the East. So far theologians have been studying the methodological issues relating to religious dialogue, the nature of revelation, and the meaning of salvation in the non-Christian religions. But see, for example, C.S. Song, *The Compassionate God* (Maryknoll, N.Y.: Orbis Books, 1982); and Swami Abhishiktananda, *Saccidananda: A Christian Approach to Advaitic Experience* (Delhi: I.S.P.C.K., 1974).

3. Karl Rahner, *Foundations of Christian Faith,* trans. William Dych (New York: Seabury Press, 1978), pp. 176–321. Hans Urs von Balthasar, *The von Balthasar Reader,* ed. Medard Kehl and Werner Löser, trans. Robert J. Daly and Fred Lawrence (New York: Crossroad Publishing Co., 1982), pp. 113–204; and also *The Glory of the Lord,* Vol. 1: *Seeing the Form,* trans. Erasmo Leiva-Merikakis (Edinburgh: T. & T. Clark, 1982), especially pp. 429–525.

4. Hans Küng, *On Being a Christian,* trans. Edward Quinn (Garden City, New York: Doubleday & Co., 1976).

5. Monika K. Hellwig, *Jesus—The Compassion of God* (Wilmington, Del: Michael Glazier, Inc., 1983). "To be a fol-

lower of Jesus," she writes, "means in the first place to enter by compassion into his experience, with all that it expresses of the divine and of the human. And it means in the second place to enter with him into the suffering and the hope of all human persons, making common cause with them as he does, and seeking out as he does the places of his predilection among the poor and despised and oppressed" (p. 108). See especially pp. 109–123.

6. Sebastian Moore, *The Crucified Jesus Is No Stranger* (New York: Seabury Press, 1977), pp. 18–20.

7. Many theologians today insist that Jesus' resurrection has to be the starting point for Christological reflection. See, for example, Chapter 3 of Wolfhart Pannenberg, *Jesus—God and Man,* trans. Lewis Wilkins and Duane Priebe (Philadelphia: Westminster Press, 1968), and Frans Jozef van Beeck, *Christ Proclaimed* (New York: Paulist Press, 1979).

8. For example, see Albert Nolan, *Jesus Before Christianity* (Maryknoll, N.Y.: Orbis Books, 1978).

9. John F. O'Grady, *Models of Jesus* (New York: Doubleday & Co., 1981).

10. John B. Cobb, Jr., *Christ in a Pluralistic Age* (Philadelphia: Westminster Press, 1975); Lewis S. Ford, *The Lure of God* (Philadelphia: Fortress Press, 1978), pp. 45–97; David R. Griffin, *A Process Christology* (Westminster Press, 1973). On the need to include an evolutionary perspective in Christological thinking, see Eugene TeSelle, *Christ in Context* (Fortress Press, 1975), pp. 127–169.

11. See Milan Machoveč, *A Marxist Looks at Jesus* (Philadelphia: Fortress Press, 1976); and José Miranda, *Being and the Messiah,* trans. John Eagleson (Maryknoll, N.Y.: Orbis Books, 1977).

12. Peter C. Hodgson, *Jesus—Word and Presence* (Philadelphia: Fortress Press, 1971).

13. See, for instance, Norman Perrin, *A Modern Pilgrimage in New Testament Christology* (Philadelphia: Fortress Press, 1974), pp. 104–121; Paul J. Achtemeier, *Mark* (Fortress Press,

1975), pp. 41–50; and Jack Kingsbury, *The Christology of Mark's Gospel* (Fortress Press, 1983).

14. John's Christology can be culled from a number of commentaries on the Fourth Gospel. In particular, see Raymond E. Brown, *The Gospel According to John,* 2 vols. (New York: Doubleday & Co., 1966 and 1970). Also, see James D.G. Dunn, *Unity and Diversity in the New Testament* (Philadelphia: Westminster Press, 1977), pp. 203–231; and Edward Schillebeeckx, *Christ: The Experience of Jesus as Lord,* trans. John Bowden (New York: Seabury Press, 1980), pp. 305–432.

15. See Gerald O'Collins, *Interpreting Jesus* (New York: Paulist Press, 1983), pp. 5–6; also, Geoffrey Wainwright, *Doxology: The Praise of God in Worship, Doctrine, and Life* (New York: Oxford University Press, 1980), pp. 45–86.

16. See James D.G. Dunn, *Jesus and the Spirit* (Philadelphia: Westminster Press, 1975), and G.W.H. Lampe, *God as Spirit* (Oxford: Oxford University Press, 1977).

17. Walter Kasper writes: "Compared with the total Christological witness of Scripture, the Christological dogma of Chalcedon represents a contraction. The dogma is exclusively concerned with the inner constitution of the divine and human subject. It separates this question from the total context of Jesus' history and fate, from the relation in which Jesus stands, not only to the *Logos* but to 'his Father', and we miss the total eschatological perspective of biblical theology" (*Jesus the Christ,* trans. V. Green [New York: Paulist Press, 1976], p. 238).

18. *The Christian Faith in the Doctrinal Documents of the Catholic Church,* ed. J. Neuner and J. Dupuis (Westminster, Md.: Christian Classics, 1975), p. 148.

19. See James D.G. Dunn, *Christology in the Making* (Philadelphia: Westminster Press, 1980), pp. 98–128.

20. For a fuller discussion of these ideas in the light of Paul's theology, I highly recommend Jerome Murphy-O'Connor, *Becoming Human Together* (Wilmington, Delaware: Michael Glazier, Inc., 1982). See pp. 70–85 and pp. 98–101. Writing

about the freedom of Jesus, Gerald Sloyan remarked: "It would be a tragic commentary on our race if someone who seemed so completely free in his humanity were to be hailed for it as more than a man" [see *Jesus In Focus* (Mystic, Conn.: Twenty-Third Publications, 1983), p. 67]. At the risk of oversimplifying an important element of the Christian message, perhaps we should be explaining to people that the difference between us and Jesus does not consist primarily of the fact that he is God and we are not. Rather, the difference is that Jesus was in full possession of his humanness—that is, he was fully free, fully alive to the Father's reign in his life—and we are not, at least not yet.

21. *Foundations of Christian Faith,* p. 104.

22. Another way of describing purity of heart is to speak of the heart's vision. In explaining a point made by Nicholas of Cusa, John S. Dunne writes in *The Reasons of the Heart* (New York: Macmillan Publishing Co., 1978): "our seeing of God consists of our having a sense of God seeing us: to see God is to see one who sees; it is to have an experience of being seen" (p. 39). And again: "One does not see God, but at most sees what God sees. It is perhaps sharing in God's own vision of the world" (p. 44). Another way of speaking about the sinlessness of Jesus might be to say that Jesus revealed God's passion for human beings. Jesus both received the outpouring of God's love for him and returned it. Rosemary Haughton writes: "The nature of God is love, and the origin of love, the Father from whom is life, pours himself out in total giving in the Beloved, who, in his human nature, receives the outpouring of love, and receives it *as human,* that is, as coinherent in all human life and in all creation. Therefore (since sin is the condition in which created life *is*) he receives it in a condition which 'blocks' the flow of love in return. . . . The cry of Jesus on the cross at the very end was, therefore, the cry of awareness that all indeed was accomplished, brought to its consummation. He knew that he could, at last, give back to the One he loved the unshackled fullness of love, and in so doing *carry with him* on the surge of that passion

the love which is the essential being of all creation" (*The Passionate God* [New York: Paulist Press, 1981], p. 153).

2. Do I Have a Soul Worth Saving?

1. Origen, *Homilies on Genesis and Exodus,* trans. Ronald E. Heine (*The Fathers of the Church,* Vol. 71 [Washington, D.C.: Catholic University of America Press, 1982], p. 47).

2. St. Augustine, *The Literal Meaning of Genesis,* Vol. 1, trans. John Hammond Taylor (*Ancient Christian Writers,* No. 41 [New York: Paulist Press, 1982], p. 25).

3. See Jurgen Moltmann's essay "Creation as an Open System" in his book *The Future of Creation,* trans. Margaret Kohl (Philadelphia: Fortress Press, 1979).

4. Pierre Teilhard de Chardin, *Hymn of the Universe,* trans. Gerald Vann (New York: Harper & Row, 1969), pp. 84–85.

5. Another way of stating this would be to say, with Karl Rahner, that eternity arises from within time, for eternity is the mature fruit of freedom. See *Foundations of Christian Faith,* trans. William Dych (New York: Seabury Press, 1978), pp. 271–274, 435–441.

6. John S. Dunne writes: "Why does being capable of love depend, therefore, on being willing to go through suffering? It is because loving means going out to the things of life just as knowing means taking them into oneself. When I make the lover's choice, when I give my heart to my life rather than withhold my heart, I enter into a relationship with the things of my life that makes me vulnerable in loving the world, 'for God so loved the world . . .' So if I am unwilling to go through suffering, I become unable to make the lover's choice. If I enter into God's relationship with the world, on the other hand, if I embrace suffering, that of my own life and that of others in its connection with me, I become able to give my heart. I become capable of love and of the knowledge that comes of love. I become capable

of God" (*The Church of the Poor Devil* [Notre Dame, Ind.: University of Notre Dame Press, 1983], p. 121).

7. St. Augustine, *Confessions,* Book 1:7, trans. R.S. Pine-Coffin (New York: Penguin Books, 1961; 1981), pp. 27–28.

8. In commenting on the tension between spirit and flesh in Romans 7, James D.G. Dunn noted that "the warfare does not end when the Spirit comes; on the contrary, that is when it really begins." (See *Jesus and the Spirit* [Philadelphia: Westminster Press, 1975], pp. 314–315.)

3. Who Owns the Future?

1. The reader who would appreciate some additional reflection on the Christian understanding of the future might want to consult Walter Kasper, *Faith and the Future,* trans. Robert Nowell (New York: Crossroad Publishing Co., 1982), pp. 1–27, 52–63.

2. See Gerald O'Collins, *What Are They Saying about the Resurrection?* (New York: Paulist Press, 1978), and *The Resurrection of Jesus Christ* (Valley Forge, Pa.: The Judson Press, 1973). Also, Michael Cook, *The Jesus of Faith* (New York: Paulist Press, 1981), pp. 73–99, and Hans Küng, *Eternal Life,* trans. Edward Quinn (Garden City, New York: Doubleday & Co., 1984), pp. 96–118.

3. Carl Sagan, *Cosmos* (New York: Random House, 1980). The captions under the illustrations read as follows: "Several billion years from now there will be a last perfect day. Then, over a period of millions of years, the Sun will swell, the Earth will heat, many lifeforms will be extinguished, and the shoreline will retreat. The oceans will rapidly evaporate, and the atmosphere will escape to space. As the Sun evolves toward a red giant, the Earth will become dry, barren, and airless. Eventually the sun will fill most of the sky, and may engulf the earth" (pp. 228–229).

4. "It is then understandable, further, that Jesus' resurrection was not seen as a private Easter for his private Good Friday,

Notes

but as the beginning and source of the abolition of the universal Good Friday, of that god-forsakenness of the world which comes to light in the deadliness of the death of the cross. Hence the resurrection of Christ was not understood merely as the first instance of a general resurrection of the dead and as a beginning of the revelation of the divinity of God in the non-existent, but also as the source of the risen life of all believers and as a confirmation of the promise which will be fulfilled in all and will show itself in the very deadliness of death to be irresistible" (Jürgen Moltmann, *Theology of Hope*, trans. James W. Leitch [New York: Harper & Row, 1967], p. 211).

5. Willi Marxsen, *Mark the Evangelist*, trans. James Boyce, Donald Juel, and William Poehlmann (Nashville: Abingdon Press, 1969), pp. 93–94.

6. William Johnston, ed., *The Cloud of Unknowing* (Garden City, New York: Doubleday Image Books, 1973), chapter 60, p. 127.

Appendix: Catholic and Christian

1. Karl Rahner, *The Practice of Faith* (New York: The Crossroad Publishing Co., 1983), pp. 13–14.

2. Wolfhart Pannenberg, *The Church*, trans. Keith Crim (Philadelphia: The Westminster Press, 1983), pp. 9–22.

3. Bernard Cooke, "Non-Patriarchal Salvation," *Horizons* 10:1 (1983), 22–31. Also, see Elisabeth Schüssler Fiorenza, *In Memory of Her* (New York: Crossroad Publishing Co., 1983), pp. 118–154.